Praise for *The Power of Equivocation*

"Complexity, ambiguity, tensions, paradox, multiplicity. The Hebrew Bible is comfortable with all of these, so why aren't we? As a feminist, Jewish interpreter Amy Kalmanofsky helps us see and appreciate the complexities and ambiguities in a number of engaging interpretations of biblical stories of female characters. But she also helps us to be aware of the complexity of us as readers and the multiple roles and identities that impact what we see, or do not see, in the text and in the world. We need this book on equivocal readings of the Hebrew Bible now more than ever, as we, individually and collectively, struggle to regain our footing in a post-pandemic world in which uncertainty and insecurity have become the new normal."

—L. Juliana Claassens, Stellenbosch University

"*The Power of Equivocation* is a thoughtful, generous, and deeply feminist reimagining of what it means to read the Bible. Kalmanofsky takes on the contradictions and moral complexities of biblical narrative and makes them the centerpiece of 'equivocal reading,' an interpretive practice that is at once flexible, critical, and affirming. A book for all biblical readers. An *un*equivocal success."

—Rhiannon Graybill, Rhodes College

"A joy to read for all who welcome questions more than answers. Kalmanofsky has curated rich readings for those who recognize openly that we inevitably bring our complex selves to a beautifully complex text."

—Brittany N. Melton, Palm Beach Atlantic University and University of the Free State

"Kalmanofsky's latest work is committed to revealing the intentional ambiguities of biblical storytelling, while also acknowledging the complexities of reading the Hebrew Bible as a scholar, a feminist, and a Jew. She adeptly strikes a balance between the personal and the useful that is often elusive for scholars. Following her through some of the most well-known biblical tales and marveling at her illumination of their many complexities was akin to reading a comprehensive travel guide of your hometown: Who knew there was so much to see in something so familiar?"

—Stephen Wilson, Georgetown University

THE POWER OF
EQUIVOCATION

THE
POWER OF
EQUIVOCATION

Complex Readers and Readings of the
Hebrew Bible

AMY KALMANOFSKY

FORTRESS PRESS
Minneapolis

THE POWER OF EQUIVOCATION
Complex Readers and Readings of the Hebrew Bible

Cover design: Kristin Miller
Cover image: Jean Metzinger, *Deus Nus*, 1910–11

Print ISBN: 978-1-5064-7871-5
eBook ISBN: 978-1-5064-7872-2

To my בית נאמן*, unequivocally*

CONTENTS

ACKNOWLEDGMENTS

This book is deeply rooted in who I am. I am grateful to the family, friends, and colleagues who have shaped me as a scholar, a Jew, and a woman. I am particularly grateful to the people who have shared the classroom with me—my teachers and my students. Throughout my life, I have been enormously fortunate to inhabit educational and religious spaces that are open and tolerant, that are defined more by questions asked than answers given, and that understand that intellectual rigor only enriches religious meaning.

I am extremely thankful that I developed as a scholar, a teacher, and a Jew at the Jewish Theological Seminary (JTS). JTS has nurtured my critical and religious languages, helping me to perceive and appreciate the timeless and the time-bound in what I study. Above all, JTS cultivates classrooms that embrace complexity—classrooms in which Bible and Torah flourish and in which students strive to understand what they study while they make meaning from it.

I have no doubt that these classrooms and students contribute to the rich and complex interpretive tradition of the Hebrew Bible and will ensure its future. This book grew from those classrooms and students. I am indebted to them for what they have given me and grateful for what I know they will give to others for generations to come.

EQUIVOCAL READINGS OF THE HEBREW BIBLE

An Introduction from an Equivocal Reader

Academics write books that reflect personal talents and interests and that potentially carry them up the career ladder. With each book, an academic's voice grows looser. Unsurprisingly, job security sows confidence that enables one to pursue ideas that are less well-traveled or are more innovative or even controversial. It also fosters a willingness to reveal one's self and biases more openly.

This is my fourth book and my most personal. It comes from a desire to address who I am as a reader and scholar of the Hebrew Bible. At its core, it is a book about complexity—the Bible's complexity. But it is also a book that reflects the complexity I bring as a reader to this inherently complex text. I am a complicated reader of the Hebrew Bible. I read the Bible as a Jew, a feminist, and a scholar. Depending on the context, I may foreground differently which persona I present first, yet all three perspectives are integral to who I am and inform how I engage with the Bible.

To admit this in a book intended for a wide range of readers, including scholars, is unsettling. Scholars rarely own so much subjectivity—or perhaps the kind of subjectivity that admits a religious orientation. For some, it would be better that I admit that I read the Bible more as a woman than as a Jew. After all, my femaleness connects me to more people and is arguably more integral to who I am. Saying I read the Bible as a woman seems more like an *objective* truth than saying I read as a Jew.

In the world I inhabit, in which secularism is more the norm, my religious affiliation is a matter of personal choice. For me, it is precisely the choice to read as a Jew that makes it an essential part of my identity. I cannot help but read the Bible as a woman, since it is the most natural and all-encompassing part of my identity. But I actively choose to read as a Jew, and therefore, I must decide what that means and how my relationship to the Bible relates to my identity as a Jew. More precisely, I must consider how my Judaism impacts my scholarship, which has focused on gender construction in the Bible. I have come to believe that there is an inherent tension in reading the Bible as a scholar—particularly a feminist scholar—and as a Jew. This book is my effort to address and embrace this tension.

At its heart, this is a book about complexity. It derives from a need to address my contradictory impulses as a reader (which I outline later on), but it focuses in the main on the intricacy of the Bible. Without question, the Bible is a literarily complicated book on the macro- and microlevels. On the macrolevel, the Bible is a book of books that spans literary genres and was composed and edited over generations. On the microlevel, each narrative also comprises different literary genres and reveals its own editorial history. Poetry interrupts prose. Law interrupts narrative. A narrative includes contradictory details. Certainly at the editorial level, both macro and micro, the Bible is not uncomfortable with contradiction or inconsistency. The Bible incorporates two variations of a creation story[1] and different calculations for the length of the primordial flood,[2] as well as different calculations of the time Israel spent enslaved in Egypt.[3]

The Bible also presents different theological ideologies, allowing the transcendence of Deuteronomy to coexist with the immanence of Leviticus. These inconsistencies may be tolerated by an editor who was interested in preserving distinct traditions. Yet the traditions are not marked as distinct. The lack of self-consciousness in merging them even within one narrative, suggests a literary tolerance for discord that is foreign to a contemporary reader. Contemporary readers are not comfortable with a character or a place

---

1 See Gen 1–2:25.

2 Gen 7:17 records that the flood lasted 40 days. Gen 7:24 records 150 days.

3 Gen 15:13 records that Israel will spend 400 years enslaved. Exod 12:40 records 430 years of enslavement.

having two different names.[4] We are not comfortable with narratives that do not conform to the norms of behavior set by the text itself.[5] Or with dead characters that are mentioned as if still alive.[6]

The Bible is comfortable with narrative and ideological inconsistencies and, I argue, welcomes them. The fundamental assumption of this book is that the Bible encompasses a complexity that extends well beyond its composition. It is rhetorically, ideologically, and theologically complex. The Bible is meant to be interpreted and does not strive to be univocal. In fact, I assert that the Bible *intends* to be polyvalent and welcomes inconsistencies and employs minimal verbosity in order to be expansive in meaning.

The Bible does not advocate for a theological fundamentalism. It does not tell simple moral tales or present one-dimensional heroes or villains. Instead, the Bible relies on inconsistencies and ambiguities to construct rich and complicated narratives that engage readers. My goal is to reveal the complexity inherent in the biblical narratives I analyze and consider how I, in particular, and other readers might address them.

As readers, we should be comfortable with the Bible's elasticity and not strive to view its stories or characters as consistent in form or meaning. We also should be comfortable with its ambiguity and not expect the Bible to expose its narrative, ideological, or theological hands. It does not. In fact, I assert that the Bible is intentionally ambiguous in order to be open to a variety of meanings and to engage its readers in interpretation.[7]

Unlike biblical stories, contemporary stories are rich with physical and psychological details that reveal the characters' implicit and explicit thoughts, feelings, and motives. The characters in contemporary stories appear fuller and more rounded than biblical

---

4 Moses's father-in-law is referred to as Jethro in Exod 3:1, Reuel in Exod 2:18, and Hobab in Num 10:29.

5 Jacob marries sisters Rachel and Leah in Gen 29 despite the prohibition against marrying sisters found in Lev 18:18.

6 In Gen 37:10, Jacob mentions his wife Rachel as if she was alive, although her death is recorded in Gen 35:19.

7 I employ the term *ambiguity* to indicate the possibility of multiple meanings. There are different types of ambiguity evident in the Bible such as structural, syntactic, and lexical. See Jeff Hayes, "Intentional Ambiguity in Ruth 4:5: Implications for Interpretation of *Ruth*," *JSOT* 41, no. 2 (2016): 159–82.

characters who seem flat in comparison. We know nothing about Abraham's youth and do not know how he feels or, for that matter, how Sarah feels when God commands Abraham to leave Mesopotamia and travel to Canaan. The Bible rarely provides insight into the inner life of its characters. Despite this, I do not view biblical characters or stories to be flat. Instead, I view them to be open to interpretation.

The Bible recounts less but means more. Sparse details, particularly those that illuminate the inner lives of characters, enable a range of possible understandings. Abraham may have felt frightened or sad to leave Mesopotamia. Sarah may have felt excited or angry joining him. Interpreters are free to provide these details. Similarly, biblical ambiguity and narrative inconsistencies welcome interpretation and enable a range of possibilities.

Before the documentary hypothesis took root and narrative inconsistencies were attributed to different biblical sources, generations of interpreters had to make sense of the two creation stories and the discrepancies in the duration of the flood. Whether from its terseness or inconsistency, it is the openness of biblical narrative and the possibility of a range of meanings that sustains its relevance for generations of readers. Readers often fill in the Bible's gaps, account for its inconsistencies, and debate the implications.[8]

The Bible invites what I label equivocal readings—readings that do not reach neat conclusions related to ideology or character. In this book, I offer equivocal readings of biblical narratives that

---

8 Sometimes a text itself will resolve its ambiguities, as Hayes notes, "Most ambiguous phrases are actually disambiguated by subsequent phrases." Ibid., 165. Second Chr 35:13 is a text that resolves ambiguities. Exod 12:8–9 prescribes that the Passover offering be "burned" not "boiled (בשל)." Deut 16:7 contradicts this passage by using the verb בשל to describe how the Passover offering should be prepared. Second Chr 35:13 resolves the resulting ambiguity by describing King Josiah's Passover offering as being cooked (בשל) in fire, thereby expanding the meaning of בשל to include more forms of cooking than boiling. Hayes labels phrases that remain ambiguous "persistently ambiguous." Both persistent and temporary ambiguity can be intentional. As Hayes notes, it is difficult to identify intentional ambiguity: "A key step in identifying an intentional ambiguity is identifying where and how its author disambiguates it in subsequent phrases, that is, by determining that it is a temporary rather than a persistent ambiguity. Though an author's failure to disambiguate an ambiguity does not preclude its being intentional, persistent ambiguities are much harder to identify as intentional." Ibid., 166.

embrace and reveal their complicatedness. An equivocal reading acknowledges the Bible's inconsistencies and offers different ways of understanding a story or character. Most importantly, an equivocal reading acknowledges the ways in which alternative readings are organic to a text.

From a reading of Genesis 22, it is legitimate to argue that God expects Abraham to kill his son or that God never intends Abraham to kill his son. Both readings are possible and, I argue, are tolerated and integral to the text. An equivocal reading acknowledges the limits of understanding the meaning of a text and the variety of meanings a text can have—particularly an ancient text like the Bible, in which the motives or sources of its authors and editors can never be fully recovered. An equivocal reading reveals a narrative's and character's contradictions and complexities. A biblical character like Joseph can be a flawed hero. A story like Hannah's can simultaneously empower and limit a woman.

Now I write as a Jewish feminist biblical scholar. I present equivocal readings because I believe they best reflect the style and intent of biblical narratives. Significantly, I offer equivocal readings because I am an equivocal reader of the Hebrew Bible, particularly its stories in which women have an important role.

At times, I am a generous reader who marvels at the strength and impact of the women of the Bible. Other times, I am a suspicious reader who reveals the Bible's patriarchal ideologies and strategies. Often, I am aware of both perspectives while reading a single text. In scholarly discourse—where consistency, objectivity, and overt subjectivity are prized—I generally cannot present as an equivocal reader. I must argue whether a specific narrative, or the Bible at large, works for or against its women.

Feminist biblical scholarship has definitively shown the ways in which the Hebrew Bible privileges and protects male political and social status and power at the expense of female power and status. Given this, contemporary readers of all gender orientations who embody feminist values and perspectives find it increasingly difficult to engage with biblical texts that ascribe secondary status to women,[9] that at times describe sexual violations of women, and that

---

9 Lev 27:1–8, which outlines the monetary equivalences of human vows, illustrates well the contrast between the value of a woman and the value of a man. A male aged

often protect masculine honor at women's expense.[10] It is particularly challenging for readers who also have religious orientations to these texts as I do. We are placed in the uncomfortable position of having to apologize for texts we cherish and perhaps even sanctify as canonical to our religious traditions.

Our readings of challenging texts could be seen as having been influenced by our religious beliefs and shaped by our desire to remain in relationship with these texts. We could be accused of being overly generous readers, unwilling to go far enough to condemn a sexist text.[11] For those of us whose *job* it has been to expose the values and strategies of the biblical texts that privilege masculinity and men, this is even more challenging.

We appear to value our religions over our feminism and could be viewed as working on behalf of our religious traditions despite our feminism. Even worse, our feminism could be viewed in service of our religious traditions. This is my dilemma. I feel a tension in reading the Bible as a Jew and as a woman. This makes me an equivocal reader.

Feminist biblical scholarship has been a steady and growing field of biblical studies for the past fifty years—ever since Phyllis Trible's groundbreaking article "Depatriarchalizing in Biblical

---

twenty to sixty is worth fifty shekels, while a same-age female is worth thirty. A male over sixty is worth fifteen, while a female over sixty is worth ten.

10 Dinah's story in Gen 34 can be read as a text that protects male honor at a woman's sexual expense. See Esther Fuchs, *Sexual Politics in the Biblical Narrative: Reading the Hebrew Bible as a Woman* (Sheffield, UK: Sheffield Academic, 2000), 200–224. Commenting on Dinah's brothers' reaction to Shechem's having sexually taken Dinah, Fuchs writes, "The reference to 'Jacob's daughter' implies that by offending Dinah, Shechem also offended Dinah's father and her brothers. The dignity of the family and of the Israelite nation is here at stake, not the physical and emotional aggression suffered by the girl herself." Ibid., 213–14.

11 Ayesha S. Chaudhry expresses a similar frustration in being a Muslim feminist Islamic studies scholar; she writes, "The very term *religious feminist* is seen by some as an oxymoron. *Patriarchal coreligionists*, who promote the patriarchal version of the religion; *cultural relativist liberals*, who suspend all moral judgment when approaching a culture they do not consider their own; and *supercessionist feminists*, who see religion as irredeemably patriarchal, all accuse religious feminists of 'inauthenticity' and of 'compromising' fundamental values of religion and feminism, respectively." See Chaudhry, "Naming Violence: Qur'anic Interpretation between Social Justice and Cultural Relativism," in *Sexual Violence and Sacred Texts*, ed. Amy Kalmanofsky (Cambridge: Feminist Studies in Religion Books, 2017), 95.

Interpretation" appeared in 1973.[12] Trible was joined by other academic pioneers who created the field of feminist biblical studies such as Carol Meyers, Athalya Brenner, Tikva Frymer-Kensky, Esther Fuchs, J. Cheryl Exum, and Elisabeth Schüssler Fiorenza.

I am a student of these pioneers and a beneficiary of their work. These scholars helped me secure a place within biblical studies. Their work has paved the way for my work by creating professional platforms and, more fundamentally, by helping me read the Hebrew Bible differently. Their suspicious, against-the-grain, countertraditional readings of biblical texts enabled me to remain interested in the Bible and to continue to be in relationship with it.

Despite the efforts of feminist biblical scholars to challenge traditional understandings of biblical texts, I am keenly aware of the ways in which feminist biblical scholarship's focus on problematic texts brings attention to these texts and grants them vitality. I and other scholars return again and again to the same narratives and arguably have created our own feminist biblical canon that consists of horrific stories of violence against the Bible's women.

I believe that this work is important and forever has changed the course of biblical interpretation. Yet I wonder if by continuing to engage with these texts, by reading them again and again, feminist biblical scholars in some ways perpetuate their ideology. We keep these stories alive for secular-critical readers who read the Bible as they would any other ancient text and for religious-critical readers who also relate to the Bible as a religious text.

Religious-critical readers place the Bible within its historical context and employ critical methodologies that illuminate the ways in which the Bible is a product of history and is defined by literary conventions and political and religious intentions. Feminist biblical critics expose the Bible's underbelly by baring its biased strategies and assumptions. For religious-critical readers, feminist biblical criticism affirms our values and perspectives, while allowing us to express our discontents with the Bible. Doing so enables us to remain engaged with the Bible. In this way, feminist biblical interpretation could be viewed as acting in service of religious tradition by helping make the Bible relevant to its feminist religious readers.

---

12 Phyllis Trible, "Depatriarchalizing in Biblical Interpretation," *JAAR* 41, no. 1 (1973): 30–48.

We can continue to engage with the Bible if we name its flaws and demonstrate the ways in which the Bible perpetuates a male-privileging ideology. Arguably though, feminist biblical interpretation should expose patriarchal strategies in order to depose the Bible's status as a sacred text in the western canon and in religious tradition; as J. Cheryl Exum writes, "The starting point of feminist criticism of the Bible is not the biblical texts in their own right but the concerns of feminism as a worldview and as a political enterprise. Recognizing that in the history of civilization, women have been marginalized by men and denied access of authority and influence, feminist criticism seeks to expose the strategies by which men have justified their control over women."[13] Instead, feminist biblical criticism keeps religious-critical readers engaged with this text, keeping it culturally and religiously alive for a new generation of readers.

Again, I write from a personal perspective. I am a female, liberal rabbi with a PhD in biblical studies who teaches undergraduate, graduate, and rabbinical students in a Jewish seminary. Although I grew up in a secular household, my first relationship with the Bible was as the Torah recited in a religious context.[14] While I explored and solidified my Jewish identity in college by attending religious services and studying in Israel, I read the Bible in literature classes and fell in love with its complexity and beauty.

My senior thesis applied psychoanalytic theory to the Song of Songs and argued that the Song was an adolescent expression of love. That year, I decided that I wanted to go to rabbinical school and get a PhD in biblical studies. I expressed the idea that I wanted to teach the Bible as Torah and the Torah as Bible. In other words, I wanted to combine the academic and the religious studies of the Bible.

Many years of study and teaching later, I believe that I have done just that. Most of my students relate to the Bible as a foundational text of some sort—either religiously or as part of their personal identity. My goal as a teacher is to enrich my students'

---

13 J. Cheryl Exum, "Feminist Criticism: Whose Interests Are Being Served?," in *Judges and Method: New Approaches in Biblical Studies Second Edition*, ed. Gale A. Yee (Minneapolis: Fortress, 2007), 65.

14 My use of the Hebrew Torah (meaning "instruction"), differentiated from Bible, indicates my religious relationship to the text.

relationship with the Bible by enhancing their understanding of it. I want my students to relate to the Bible, not as a religious artifact that is a relic of an ancient world, but as a text that continues to shape their values and their spirits. In this way, I straddle the academic and religious realms. I am committed to helping my students draw meaning from the Bible. I feel that a better understanding of the nature of the texts that comprise it, and the world that produced it, helps them derive greater meaning from it.

This brief autobiography provides context for me as a reader of the Bible, which I hope is instructive to other religious-critical readers. I consider myself primarily to be an interpreter of the Bible who applies the tools of contemporary critical theory and methodologies to extract meaning from this ancient text. Gender construction has been my primary focus.[15] My work exposes the Bible's gender ideology that actively undermines women's status as well as the ways in which the Bible at times undermines its own gender ideology.

Broadly, my work argues that the Bible recognizes female power and uses it in support of a male-privileging gender identity. The Bible sometimes plays with gender norms and presents strong, masculine women and weak, feminine men in service of its male-privileging ideology. The story of Deborah, Barak, Sisera, and Yael told in Judges 4 is an excellent example. My analysis argues that this story presents strong women and weak men, but it does not embrace them as an ideal. Instead, it presents them as an example of a society in crisis and in need of a new mode of leadership—the monarchy.[16] In other words, the Bible recognizes female power but views it as symptomatic of a world in chaos. This is a complicated conclusion to draw for feminist readers who want to identify and celebrate female power. I believe the Bible does identify female power but views it as dangerous and, therefore, channels it in service of its male-privileging ideology.

The Bible's recognition of female power, even threatening female power, could be viewed as a counterbalance to its male bias and, for some readers, justifies the continued attention to the Bible's sexually

---

15 Amy Kalmanofsky, *Dangerous Sisters of the Hebrew Bible* (Minneapolis: Fortress, 2014) and *Gender-Play in the Hebrew Bible: The Ways the Bible Challenges Its Gender Norms* (London: Routledge, 2017).

16 See Kalmanofsky, *Gender-Play*, 47–67.

violent texts. My work may be viewed then as complicit to a male privileging ideology, making it acceptable to read a detailed account of a woman's violation, such as that found in Jeremiah 13, as long as we see the woman as a powerful character because she's a threatening figure.[17] I take this critique seriously, particularly now.

My scholarship, which reveals the Bible's gender biases and rhetorical strategies that support those biases, feels vital to current conversations about sexual and gender-based harassment. It is important to note how cultures implicitly and explicitly inscribe sexism throughout their texts. The Bible provides an excellent opportunity to examine how a text encrypts sexism.[18] And yet my work, which identifies female power and focuses on figures who defy the Bible's gender norms, could deflect attention away from the Bible's patriarchal strategies and thereby could be of service to them by making the Bible and its women more palatable.

Arguably, my task as a feminist biblical scholar is to expose the Bible's sexism in order to depose the Bible as a sacred text. Instead, I empower the Bible's women and give them a voice within a literary context that views female power as useful but threatening. I remain committed to reading their stories again and again and to understanding how the Bible presents and uses its women. I remain committed to being in relationship with their stories and want my students to be in relationship with them as well.

My commitment, no doubt, is a product of my religious orientation. Perhaps I read the Bible more as a Jew than I do as a feminist. As a Jew, I am unable to condemn the Bible as a sexist text and

---

17 My article "The Monstrous Feminine in the Book of Jeremiah" provides an example. I examine how Jer 13 constructs a monstrous image of Israel and conclude, "The monstrous-feminine in Jeremiah is a negative figure designed like all monsters to provoke fear and disgust. She embodies Jeremiah's and his culture's perceptions of gender and reflects ancient Israel's fears of the female body and sexuality. But there can be no doubt that she also is a powerful figure. She threatens the norms of patriarchal Israel and serves as a warning to its men and women to curb their sexual desire, to behave appropriately and to avoid shame." Amy Kalmanofsky, "The Monstrous Feminine in the Book of Jeremiah," in *Jeremiah (Dis)placed: New Directions in Writing/Reading Jeremiah*, ed. A. R. Pete Diamond and Louis Stulman (New York: T&T Clark, 2011), 207.

18 For example, Harold G. Washington examines the ways the Bible may reflect and perpetuate a rape culture in "Violence and the Constructions of Gender in the Hebrew Bible: A New Historicist Approach," *BI* 5, no. 4 (1997): 324–63.

then depose or desanctify it. I also cannot erase the generations of interpretation that are the substance of my faith tradition and that do not include or, for the most part, even reflect or acknowledge women's concerns. But I am a *feminist* Jew who can offer perspective and critique on the Bible and on the interpretive tradition that has been shaped by male perspectives and concerns. In this way, I can expand biblical interpretation and enter its millennium-long tradition.

For some people, expanding the tradition by adding critical voices that expose the sexist assumptions of patriarchal texts and tradition is not enough to uproot these assumptions. They may be right. Continuing to engage with patriarchal texts may be a less effective strategy to counter sexist assumptions. Also it is admittedly difficult, if not impossible, to provide a new and critical perspective on a tradition that has a canonized body of interpretation.

New voices, let alone critical ones, are not as valued or welcomed as the ancient rabbinic voices. These ancient rabbinic voices are the substance of Judaism. Efforts to expand tradition may be fruitless. New readings can be devalued and dismissed. Still, I persist and hope that new voices will be respected for the values they profess and for the creativity they possess. Given who I am as a feminist biblical scholar and as a Jew, this is the only way forward that I see.

This book draws from the challenges I personally feel of reading as a feminist and as a Jew. These challenges come from being a critical and religious as well as a suspicious and generous reader—in other words, an equivocal reader of the Bible. I offer readings of biblical texts that feature women who work simultaneously to expose the ways in which the biblical texts empower and disempower women. I offer equivocal readings that draw complicated conclusions about characters' motivations and actions and that embrace their complexity.

I stand by my work that recognizes female power in the Bible and that addresses the ways in which the Bible uses that power to protect male interests. What makes this book different from my other work is that I make explicit how a text can be read to simultaneously bolster or diminish women's status. The text is not an either/or for me. I also, at times, reveal my own biases that impact my interpretations.

My goal is to model a way of reading that will enable other critical-religious readers to straddle their dual identities and loyalties—to read critically and generously—and to enable them to continue to be in relationship with the Bible in honest ways.

The Bible is a complicated text, and we are complicated readers. My experience of being an equivocal reader of the Bible has helped me see the Bible as an equivocal text. It is my assertion that the Bible is intentionally complicated and relies on narrative inconsistencies and ambiguities in order to draw readers to its narratives and characters.[19] The Bible seeks to be open to interpretation and a variety of meanings that reflect the complexity of its readers.[20]

The narratives I have selected focus on women connected to the monarchy—some more directly than others.[21] Chapter one examines culpability in the story of Joseph and Potiphar's wife and argues that there is no villain or hero in this story. Chapter two considers how Hannah's story conforms to and defies the Bible's patriarchal norms and expectations related to maternity. Chapter three examines the story of the powerful yet unlawful medium from En-dor who draws Samuel from the underworld to inform the disgraced King Saul of his impending death with compassion and respect.

Chapter four addresses how Queen Esther overpowers the men in her narrative, particularly Mordecai, to become the equivocal hero of her story. Chapter five considers the ways in which Tamar, like Hannah, conforms to and challenges the Bible's typical maternal narrative and how, like Esther, she is the equivocal hero of her story. Chapter six examines Bathsheba's story and argues for viewing her as a complicated figure, both vulnerable and powerful.

---

19 Hayes notes how ambiguity often is intended for a text's audience; he writes, "Most often, a narrator's audience has more information about the plot and characters than any particular character in the narrative. Consequently, an author may intend that an ambiguity be perceived by the narrator's audience but unperceived by characters within the narrative, that is, the audience is in on the joke while the characters are ignorant." Hayes, "Intentional Ambiguity," 168.

20 Hayes writes, "As interpreters, we should always be conscious of our role in interpreting ambiguities whether we find them intentional or not: interpreters continually resolve ambiguities through the interpretive process. . . . I think we should be free to adopt whichever reading an ambiguous text allows us that resolves the most interpretive dilemmas in the narrative." Ibid., 169.

21 As the wife of a courtier, Potiphar's wife may have had the most tangential relationship with the monarchy.

Although it is interesting to consider if the Bible portrays women associated with the monarchy in particularly equivocal ways, my intention in selecting these narratives is to provide my book with cohesion. I leave others to explore more deeply the Bible's depiction of women associated with the monarchy. For this project, I am interested in modeling a way of reading narratives that feature women that could be broadly applied to other biblical narratives. I do think the Bible has a particularly complex attitude toward women that makes their stories ripe for equivocal reading. Yet I also think all biblical narratives are deceptively intricate and that readers should be sensitive to these complexities.

As always, my methodology is to engage in a close reading of these selected biblical texts that is informed by contemporary critical scholarship, particularly feminist biblical scholarship. My aim is to reveal and affirm the literary and ideological complexity of the texts I analyze and to show how complexity is integral to the construction of these biblical narratives and characters.[22]

The Bible is a complicated text, and we are complicated readers of it. The complexities we have now as readers may differ from those of our ancient forbearers, but we must assume they had their own and that the Bible was as open to their interpretations that reflect their complexities as it is to ours.

From its inception, the Bible was meant to be interpreted. I believe that religious-critical readers, who have a uniquely complicated relationship with the Bible and who approach the Bible subjectively and objectively, are particularly astute observers of the Bible's complexity. Consequently, we have an important role to play in understanding and interpreting the Bible.

The Bible serves interests. It always has. These interests can be political, social, or religious, or might be confined to a particular historical, political, social, or religious reality and feel irrelevant or even offensive to contemporary readers. Other interests feel as though they cross generations and speak to general human needs and concerns that continue to resonate. Religious-critical readers recognize this.

Equivocal readers have no choice. We see what is time-bound and what is timeless about the Bible, and by seeing both, our

---

22 Hayes similarly observes how "complexities of character and plot" are "unavailable to us without ambiguities in the text." Hayes, "Intentional Ambiguity," 182.

interpretive voices provide something crucial and unique. We are honest but generous readers of the Bible. This combination serves us and all readers of the Bible well. We see the Bible's cultural limitations and the ways it transcends those limitations. Those of us who are feminist religious-critical readers see the ways the Bible protects male interests at the expense of female interests. We see how the Bible makes use of women's power but does so to bolster male power.

We expose, but we do not depose. In fact, we labor to ensure that people continue to read, interpret, and value the Bible despite its flaws, while we remain aware of them. As complicated readers, we labor to elucidate a complicated text. I hope our efforts illuminate the intricacies and richness of the Bible and engage readers who also will expand the canon of interpretation and enable future generations to remain in relationship with the Bible.

Admittedly, this may be self-deceiving or self-serving. In truth, equivocal reading may not be for everyone—not every reader happily embraces intentional ambiguity and multiplicity of meaning. Not every feminist reader allows a text to work for or against its women, and not all religious readers are willing to see the ways in which the Bible does not align with their values. Equivocal reading is not for everyone, but it is the only way for this Jewish, feminist, and critical reader of the Bible.

CHAPTER ONE

POTIPHAR'S WIFE AND JOSEPH

Biblical women and men are often complicated figures. This chapter examines two complicated biblical characters—Potiphar's wife and Joseph—and offers an equivocal reading that reveals how both characters are essential figures in their narrative and how neither character is a paradigm of vice or virtue. As I write in my introduction, equivocal readings do not seek to reach tidy conclusions related to ideology or character. Rather, they reveal the complexities of a biblical story or a character.

In general, equivocal readers find it difficult to identify heroes and villains in narratives. Recognizing complexity illuminates the flaws and weaknesses of heroes and the virtues and strengths of villains. Feminist-religious readers of the Bible have a particularly hard time identifying female heroes and villains. Our generous perspectives encourage us to celebrate the women of the Bible who impact their narratives, even when their actions often defy biblical and even contemporary norms. Our suspicious perspectives enable us to see how biblical narratives can work to limit, condemn, and sometimes vilify their women.

Alice Bach's description of "reading as a woman" captures the essence of equivocal reading. Bach notes how a feminist reader "gives voice to the female figure in the text and seeks to escape being seduced by the narrator into accepting his view."[1] By doing so, a

---

1 Alice Bach, "Breaking Free of the Biblical Frame-Up: Uncovering the Woman in Genesis 39," in *A Feminist Companion to Genesis*, ed. Athalya Brenner (Sheffield, UK: Sheffield Academic, 1998), 319.

feminist reader places female characters in relief within the context of their narratives, recognizing a depth, dimension, and strength to these characters that stands independent of, and often in contrast to, the narrator's more limiting perspective.

Whereas some feminist readers provide that depth by engaging in creative interpretation that fills in narrative gaps, others provide the depth by engaging in interpretation that relies heavily on intertextuality. As Johanna Stiebert observes, intertextuality is "a literary form of inner-biblical exegesis, whereby biblical texts are brought into relationship with and mutually illuminate each other—notably through verbal echoes."[2] Through thematic and linguistic "verbal echoes," characters and their narratives are linked, providing them with broader dimensions and greater complexity. The connection between texts frees characters from their immediate context and from the narrator's perspective and provides equivocal feminist readers more content with which to ground our interpretations within the Bible.

I consider intertextuality to be a core literary component of the Bible's artistry. Many of the equivocal readings I offer in this book rely heavily on intertextuality. This supports my general assertion that complexity is integral to biblical texts and is imported into the texts not solely by complex readers. Intertextuality, as I demonstrate, reveals the complexities of Genesis 39, which tells the story of Joseph's tenure in Potiphar's house. This story has many verbal echoes throughout the Bible that provide texture and nuance to its narrative and characters. Sold into servitude by his brothers, Joseph arrives in Egypt, where he is purchased by Potiphar, a courtier of Pharaoh. Joseph succeeds within Potiphar's household, and his good looks attract Potiphar's wife, who continuously offers herself sexually to Joseph. Joseph refuses her advances until one day he finds himself alone with her. Potiphar's wife offers herself yet again, this time grabbing hold of Joseph's garment. Joseph runs away, leaving the garment in her hand. Potiphar's wife then uses this garment to frame Joseph for rape. In response, Potiphar casts Joseph out of

---

2 Johanna Stiebert, "The Wife of Potiphar, Sexual Harassment, and False Rape Allegations: Genesis 39 in Select Social Contexts of the Past and Present," in *The Bible and Gender Troubles in Africa*, ed. J. Kügler, R. Gabaitse, and J. Stiebert (Bamberg: University of Bamberg Press, 2019), 78.

his household and places him in jail, where, yet again, Joseph rises in rank.

Traditional readings of Genesis 39 uniformly condemn Potiphar's wife and hail Joseph as a righteous man for resisting her sexual advances.[3] In prerabbinic and rabbinic literature, Potiphar's wife is viewed as the villain of the narrative whereas Joseph is seen as its hero.[4] Contemporary readings of Genesis 39 perceive greater nuance in its character portrayals. Feminist readers tend to be more forgiving of Potiphar's wife and more suspicious of the narrator's perspective. Bach observes how the text suppresses Potiphar's wife's story and isolates her by not including other female characters who could reflect or respond to her experience. Bach also notes how the story does not include the reaction of Potiphar's wife to Joseph's imprisonment, which "indicates that a woman's emotions are not central to the story."[5]

Heather A. McKay offers a forgiving reading of Genesis 39 that deflects blame away from Potiphar's wife and assigns it to Potiphar. McKay accuses Potiphar "of neglect of the managing of his household."[6] Joseph is brought into Potiphar's house as a servant yet rises to a position of authority—potentially over Potiphar's wife. According to McKay, this introduces instability to the household, which Potiphar neglects to manage and that "comes to a head in a disturbing event, a nasty scene."[7] In McKay's equivocal reading, Potiphar's wife may have behaved poorly, but her actions are understandable, even if not justified. Potiphar's wife, McKay argues, could assume that Joseph was purchased to inseminate her in lieu of her husband, who McKay views to be a eunuch.[8]

---

3 For an overview of traditional interpretation, see Shimon Bakon, "Subtleties in the Story of Joseph and Potiphar's Wife," *JBQ* 41, no. 3 (2013): 171–74.

4 Joshua Levinson writes, "In general, the dominant reading presents Joseph as a paragon of virtue and self-control, sometimes tempted but never faltering. Potiphar's wife, on the other hand, is often portrayed as driven by her passions to the point of madness." Joshua Levinson, "An-Other Woman: Joseph and Potiphar's Wife. Staging the Body Politic," *JQR* 87, nos. 3–4 (1997): 271–72.

5 Bach, "Breaking Free," 340.

6 Heather A. McKay, "Confronting Redundancy as Middle Manager and Wife: The Feisty Woman of Genesis 39," *Semeia* 87 (1999): 221.

7 Ibid., 224.

8 Ibid., 227.

Perceiving Potiphar's wife as less culpable for her actions is compelling to contemporary feminist readers who identify and address the Bible's patriarchal ideology. It is important for these readers to recognize, as Esther Fuchs does, the ways in which the Bible works to condemn Potiphar's wife for being a "married woman who seeks sexual escapades with other men." Fuchs asserts that women like this in the Bible "must be portrayed as treacherous, dangerous, lethal."[9] Feminist readers strive to break free of this patriarchal perspective and "give voice to the suppressed story of the woman," as Bach does.[10] Yet it is also important to contemporary readers to condemn acts of unwanted sexual advances, whether done by a man or a woman, and to recognize the ways Potiphar's wife abuses her power. Stiebert observes how Potiphar's wife demands sex crassly and pesters Joseph daily, and when thwarted, she "becomes angry and lies about him."[11] For these reasons, Potiphar's wife is an equivocal figure even for feminist readers, who attempt to release her from a patriarchal narrative context that portrays her as treacherous while recognizing the ways in which her behavior is reprehensible in a contemporary context.

In this chapter, I offer an equivocal reading of Genesis 39 that shows how the Bible portrays Potiphar's wife and Joseph as equivocal figures who do not fall neatly into the roles of villain and hero. In my reading, which relies on intertextuality, Joseph is not presented as a righteous figure, nor is Potiphar's wife as an evil character, as has been traditionally understood. Instead, they are complicated figures whose complexity is integral to the text and its meaning. Their story is not told to identify a hero who is rewarded for his virtue and a villain who is punished for her depravity. Rather, its purpose is to show God's design and control over events and people, despite human shortcomings and efforts to intervene. Genesis 39 is about divine providence, not human virtue.

As a result, Joseph and Potiphar's wife should be viewed as God's instruments, whose actions do not identify moral behaviors associated with righteousness and wickedness. Instead, both ensure and reflect God's plan for Joseph and his descendants. In my

---

9 Fuchs, *Sexual Politics*, 146.
10 Bach, "Breaking Free," 341.
11 Stiebert, "Wife of Potiphar," 101.

equivocal reading, Joseph is more blessed than righteous; Potiphar's wife may be more a victim of her circumstances than evil. She is also a smart and somewhat compassionate figure. Neither character should be viewed as a paragon of virtue or vice.

AN EQUIVOCAL READING OF GENESIS 39: JOSEPH'S RISE AND DEMISE

Potiphar purchases Joseph from the Ishmaelites to serve in his household, which thrives with Joseph present, as Genesis 39:2–6 describes:

> YHWH was with Joseph. He was a successful man. He was in the house of his Egyptian master. His master saw that YHWH was with him and that in all that he did, God made him succeed. Joseph found favor in his eyes. He served him and he appointed him over his household. All that he had, he placed in his hand. From the moment he appointed him over his household and all that he owned; YHWH blessed the house of the Egyptian because of Joseph. YHWH's blessing was over all that he had in the house and field. He relinquished all that he owned into Joseph's hand, paying attention only to the food he ate. Joseph was beautiful.[12]

There can be no doubt why Potiphar's household prospers. The passage states explicitly three times that the household thrives because God is with Joseph and ensures his success.

Joseph's success in Potiphar's home reflects the overall pattern of Joseph's life. Joseph learns early in his life through his dreams of sheaves and stars bowing down before him that he is destined for great things. This realization does not appeal to his brothers, who attack him in Genesis 37, intending at first to kill him but then deciding to sell him into slavery. Yet as his fate will prove, difficult situations set Joseph up for greater success, leading him ultimately to assume the position of Pharaoh's second-in-command (Gen 41:41–45). Indeed, Joseph is destined for great things.

---

12 All biblical translations are my own.

Notably, the passage describes Joseph specifically as successful (מצליח) and beautiful. He is not labeled righteous like Noah (Gen 6:9), who finds favor with and, therefore, salvation from God. Nor is he described as God-fearing like Abraham in Genesis 22:12, who earns God's blessing. Noah and Abraham have virtues that God rewards. In contrast, Joseph does not display virtues. He certainly has not displayed any righteousness up to this point in the narrative. He maligns his brothers in Genesis 37:2 and irritates them by relaying the dreams of his grandeur in Genesis 37:5. Therefore, there is no textual evidence for viewing Joseph's success in Potiphar's household as a reward for his righteousness. Joseph succeeds because God favors him and causes him to succeed, not because he is particularly worthy.[13] Joseph simply, and perhaps inexplicably, is blessed.[14]

In essential ways, Joseph's story mirrors Israel's story of success because God causes the success. Israel's release from slavery and the triumph over Egypt at the Reed Sea display God's greatness—not Israel's.[15] In fact, God's selection of and concern for Israel (the smallest nation) appears arbitrary, as Deuteronomy 7:7 declares—and perhaps it is even undeserved, as its rebellious and ungrateful behavior in the wilderness after its liberation suggests.[16] Similarly, Joseph's success in Potiphar's household and, ultimately, his elevation in Pharaoh's court to second-in-command display God's greatness, not Joseph's. Joseph's success, like Israel's, also may be undeserved.

Potiphar recognizes the blessings Joseph brings and utilizes him for his own advantage. He places Joseph in charge of his home and his field because he wants Joseph's blessings to enrich his household.

---

13 Elsewhere in the Bible, the use of the verb "to succeed [צלח]" indicates that God is guiding events. See Gen 24:42; Ps 37:7; and 1 Chr 22:11.

14 Joseph's beauty is another sign of blessing, as Stuart Macwilliam notes. Macwilliam also observes how divine favor "is heavily emphasized at the beginning and end of chapter 39, framing the narrative of injustice and misfortune that is triggered by Joseph's beauty." Stuart Macwilliam, "Ideologies of Male Beauty and the Hebrew Bible," *BI* 17, no. 3 (2009): 274.

15 God liberates Israel from Egypt with great acts that display God's strength to Egypt and Israel. See Exod 6:6–9; 14:15–18, 30–31.

16 Israel's unworthiness is evident during its liberation when the liberated slaves express their desire to return to slavery in Egypt. In response, Moses orders Israel to be silent and to witness God's act of deliverance. Exod 14:11–13.

Blessings in the Bible are measurable. Deuteronomy 28 provides many examples of these tangible blessings. Paramount among them is fertility—fertility of the womb, of livestock, and of the land (Deut 28:11). Potiphar may want all three types of fertility, but he may need Joseph most for fertility of the womb. Potiphar is identified as a *saris* (סרים), which may indicate that he is a eunuch.[17] McKay differentiates between a eunuch castrated before puberty and, therefore, "sterile and incapable of sexual arousal and a eunuch castrated after having had significant sexual experience and, therefore, capable of achieving successful sexual congress, though sterile."[18]

McKay perceives Potiphar to be "a eunuch castrated after puberty who was somewhat of a *mucho pomposo* superintendent of the guard."[19] Recognizing that the narrative does not explicate Potiphar's motives, McKay raises the possibility that Joseph was purchased to impregnate Potiphar's wife.[20] Pirson similarly assumes that it was "Potiphar's idea to bring Joseph to them, so that he could sleep with his master's wife, and therefore, considering Potiphar's physical condition, to father a child with her."[21] These assumptions about Potiphar's sexual functioning and intention provide context for what happens in his household. They also support a more generous assessment of Potiphar's wife by providing a rationale for her actions.

For Pirson, Joseph is supposed to fill a role similar to Hagar, Bilhah, and Zilpah—the handmaids of Genesis. This role would make Joseph's status below Potiphar's wife in the household's hierarchy. Yet Potiphar appears to have ceded complete oversight of his household to Joseph, paying attention only to the food he eats and not, as the inclusion of this detail makes clear, his wife. McKay suggests that Potiphar's blind eye to all but his food indicates a "laissez-faire attitude to the running of his household" that could be an abdication of his duties as head of the house.[22]

---

17 Ron Pirson remarks on the uncertainty of the meaning of *saris* as "eunuch." See Ron Pirson, "The Twofold Message of Potiphar's Wife," *Scandinavian Journal of the Old Testament* 18, no. 2 (2004): 253.

18 McKay, "Confronting Redundancy," 217.

19 Ibid., 217.

20 Ibid., 223.

21 Pirson, "Twofold Message," 256.

22 McKay, "Confronting Redundancy," 223.

For McKay, Potiphar's domestic negligence makes his wife less culpable for the events described in Genesis 39:7–9:

> After these things, his master's wife sets her eyes on Joseph. She says: "Lie with me." He refused and said to his master's wife: "Indeed, with me in the house, my master thinks of nothing. Everything that belongs to him, he has placed in my hand. No one is more important in this house than I. He has withheld from me nothing except for you, since you are his wife. How can I do this terrible thing and sin against God?"

In my reading, the mention that time passes before Potiphar's wife notices Joseph challenges the notion that Joseph was brought into the household to impregnate Potiphar's wife. If he was, it would make sense that she would approach him immediately and that Joseph would comply with her advances, assuming he knew why he was brought into the household. Instead, the passage of time and Joseph's refusal suggest that she becomes genuinely attracted to him even without any indication that her attraction is, or that her advances would be, reciprocated. Recognizing this, my argument, in contrast to McKay's, holds Potiphar's wife responsible for her encounter with Joseph. Her actions stem from her desire for Joseph and not from her husband's expectations of the role Joseph will fulfill in the household.

When Potiphar's wife notices Joseph, she immediately propositions him and commands him to lie with her (שכבה עמי). This is not a seduction but a demand for sexual relations, which readers across generations could condemn. To contemporary ears her words are reprehensible, if not criminal. She demands sex from a servant in her household, and therefore, she should be viewed as abusing her power, as Stiebert observes. Ancient readers of the Bible would have condemned Potiphar's wife for different reasons, as Stiebert also notes. They would have condemned her for being a sexually aggressive, non-Israelite woman and not for abusing her station over a subordinate.[23]

---

23 Noting that not all "sexually forward women incite outrage or disgust," Stiebert notes that foreign women in particular are condemned for being lascivious in the Bible. Stiebert, "Wife of Potiphar," 87–88.

Potiphar's wife's command to Joseph to lie with her (שכבה עמי) has interesting verbal echoes that indicate her culpability and work further to condemn her. First, the command echoes within the story in Genesis 19 of Lot's daughters who sleep with their father after the destruction of Sodom and Gomorrah from which they flee. Like Potiphar's wife, Lot's daughters are sexually aggressive. Thinking that they are the only survivors after the cataclysm, the daughters conspire to sleep with their father to preserve his patriline, using phrasing that evokes Potiphar's wife's command to Joseph ([נשכבה עמו] Gen 19:32). The daughters' efforts effectively cut their family off from Israel by producing heirs that are the progenitors of two foreign nations, the Moabites and the Ammonites—two nations that the Bible prohibits Israelites from marrying (Deut 23:4).

Potiphar's wife's command to Joseph (שכבה עמי) also reverberates with another story of inappropriate sexual assertiveness—the story of David's daughter Tamar who is raped by her half brother Amnon in 2 Samuel 13. Under false pretenses of being ill, Amnon lures Tamar into his bedroom, where he grabs hold of her and demands that she lie with him ([שכבי עמי] 2 Sam 13:11). The reverberations of Potiphar's wife's demand for sex with these two stories of sexual misconduct, in which proper relationships and their hierarchies are violated, signal her culpability and support in viewing Joseph as an innocent victim.

Stiebert observes other links between 2 Samuel 13 and the Joseph narrative. Perhaps the most direct is that Tamar and Joseph are the only people in the Bible described as wearing special tunics (כתנת פסים), both of which are torn apart.[24] Also, both Joseph and Tamar are described as beautiful (Gen 39:6; 2 Sam 13:1). For Stiebert, these echoes link the characters of Joseph and Tamar and support viewing them both as tragic victims of "powerful sexual predators" who are "entirely innocent and virtuous."[25]

Whether initiated by a male or a female, inappropriate sexual assertiveness does link the stories of Lot's daughters, Potiphar's wife, and Amnon and Tamar and may work to incriminate Potiphar's wife. Yet as an equivocal reader, I identify a crucial difference that

---

24 Ibid., 79.

25 Stiebert further observes, "Because Joseph is male and YHWH is with him, he can escape sexual violation." Ibid., 84.

separates Genesis 39 from these other biblical stories and leaves room for a more generous assessment of Potiphar's wife: her demand for sex is not met. Joseph refuses her advances. Remarkably, as I will mention later, Potiphar's wife's actions have no consequences for *her*. Despite being, in Stiebert's view, a "powerful sexual predator," she is not punished. This suggests that Potiphar, and perhaps the biblical narrator, does not hold her accountable for her sexual misconduct.

There are echoes with other biblical narratives—namely, the three wife-sister stories related in Genesis, which, in my reading, also deflect blame from Potiphar's wife and support an equivocal reading of her character.[26] In these wife-sister stories, the patriarchs Abraham and Isaac attempt to pass off their wives as their sisters while traveling in foreign territory. As Abraham makes clear to Sarah in Genesis 12:13, the ruse is intended for his own benefit and protection so that powerful foreigners do not kill him in order to claim his beautiful wife. Indeed, foreign rulers are attracted to the matriarchs. First, Sarah catches the eye of Pharaoh in Egypt, then of Abimelech in Gerar. Later, Rebecca also catches the eye of Abimelech. Once the foreign rulers understand that the women are married, they release them with gifts that enrich the patriarchs' households.

Genesis 39 and the wife-sister stories share vocabulary that suggests thematic connections. To begin, Joseph (Gen 39:6), Sarah (Gen 12:11), and Rebecca (Gen 26:7) are all described as beautiful. Their beauty brings potential danger to the beautiful characters but also, and perhaps more importantly, to those who observe their beauty and are attracted to them, as Macwilliam observes.[27] Also, Joseph's words of refusal particularly echo the vocabulary of the wife-sister story told in Genesis 20. In Genesis 39:9, Joseph refuses Potiphar's wife and claims that Potiphar has withheld (חשׂך) nothing from him except his wife and that he does not want to commit a great (גדלה) evil and sin (חטאתי) against God. In Genesis 20, Abimelech, the king of Gerar, takes Sarah into his home. Confronted

---

26 Gen 12:10–20; 20; 26:6–11.

27 Macwilliam writes, "The reader today may consider that it is the beautiful woman who is vulnerable, but it is a common theme in the Hebrew Bible that the one at risk is the gazing male. . . . Beauty as a snare for the unwary gazer lies behind the warning of Prov. 6:25 and 31:30." Macwilliam, "Ideologies of Male Beauty," 270.

by God in a dream, Abimelech declares his innocence, which God affirms in Genesis 20:6, saying, "I prevented [אחשך] you from sinning against me [מחטו לי]." Later, Abimelech confronts Abraham and asks what sin he has committed against Abraham such that Abraham brought upon him and his household a great sin (חטאה גדלה).

Perhaps most importantly, Genesis 39 tells a story, similar overall to the wife-sister narratives, of a beautiful Israelite in a foreign household who draws sexual attention. What distinguishes Genesis 39 most from the wife-sister stories is the gender of its characters. In the wife-sister stories, the attractive Israelite is female and the attracted foreigner is male. In the Joseph story, the Israelite is male and the foreigner is female. Significantly, for my equivocal reading of Potiphar's wife's character, the male foreign ruler is innocent of wrongdoing in the wife-sister stories, as God's affirmation of Abimelech makes clear. In Genesis 20:6, God acknowledges Abimelech's pure intentions.[28]

Given the parallels in both the details and the contour of the stories, it is logical to assume that Potiphar's wife might be similarly blameless for being attracted to the handsome Israelite, especially if Joseph's role in the household is to impregnate her, as McKay and Pirson suggest. Yet as Fuchs notes, Potiphar's wife's gender complicates matters, since the Bible manifests a double standard regarding polygamous tendencies. A man can have more than one sexual partner, but a woman can have only one.[29] Potiphar's wife, therefore, could be condemned for seeking a second sexual partner in Joseph. As an equivocal reader, I acknowledge this double standard.

Yet Joseph refuses her advances, thereby preventing her from committing this wrong. In this way, Potiphar's wife is like Abimelech, who is prevented from sleeping with another man's wife.

---

28 Commenting on the wife-sister stories, Fuchs writes, "Yet the Genesis scenes do not portray the monarch as an outright villain. His actions are not only explained but to some extent justified. He is shown to act out of ignorance rather than malice. It is implied that he takes another's wife because he is misinformed about her uxorial status." Fuchs, *Sexual Politics*, 125.

29 Fuchs writes, "Had Potiphar seduced one of his maids, it is doubtful that the biblical narrative would have bothered to refer to the incident let alone condemn it. Potiphar's wife is condemned because as a married woman she must not have sexual access to any man other than her husband." Ibid., 146.

As I stated previously, Joseph succeeds because God causes him to succeed; it is possible that God directs Joseph and causes him to refuse. If so, then God protects Potiphar's wife, as he did Abimelech in Genesis 20, and prevents her from sinning. The fact that she bears no consequences for her actions supports this reading. Potiphar's wife, therefore, should not be viewed as a villain in this narrative. At most, she is an equivocal figure. Indeed, she has suspect drives from the Bible's perspective, but she does not commit a crime. Joseph, or God through Joseph, prevents her from committing this crime.

Also, if God directs Joseph, then his refusal does not indicate his righteousness. He becomes a passive character whose actions are directed by God and not by his own moral compass. In fact, his words reveal more pragmatism than righteousness. Joseph does not say that he does not want to have sex with his master's wife or that adultery is a sin he refuses to commit. Rather, Joseph bases his refusal on loyalty to his master, who has given him so much and denied him so little—only his wife. Also, with his typical hubris, Joseph makes sure that Potiphar's wife knows that no one has a greater status in Potiphar's home than he does. Given this, the great sin against God he fears to commit could be ingratitude to Potiphar or even to God, who Joseph may realize is guiding his success. Joseph does not want to jeopardize his standing within the household or his receiving of God's blessings.

JOSEPH'S DEMISE AND RISE

Potiphar's wife does not take no for an answer and continues to harass Joseph, who continues to refuse her until one day she finds herself alone in her house with Joseph. This time, she grabs him by his clothes and propositions him. He flees, leaving his clothes in her hands. In Genesis 39:14–15, we read,

> She called to the members of her household and said to them: "Look, he brought for us this Hebrew man to mock us. He came to me to lie with me, but I cried out with a great cry. When he heard me raise my voice and cry, he left his clothing with me and fled outside."

Contemporary readers are likely to condemn Potiphar's wife for a second crime. Not only does she abuse her power by seducing a servant, but she now accuses him falsely of rape. To a contemporary reader, her accusation seems gratuitous. She could have discarded Joseph's clothes and kept the incident private, since they were alone in the house.[30]

Once again, an equivocal reading allows for complexity in understanding a character's motivations. Potiphar's wife's actions are more comprehensible, if not justified, in their biblical context. Afraid that someone will tell what happened—perhaps even Joseph, who the reader knows is a proven tattletale[31]—she must protect herself. After all, adultery is a capital offense in the Bible,[32] as it was in ancient Egypt. She does not want to be accused of sexually pursuing Joseph. To protect herself, she must incriminate Joseph. She also may want to remove him from the household to prevent further encounters.

Her recounting of the incident to the members of the household is notable for the details she provides and then for their differences when she later describes the event to Potiphar. An equivocal reading of her account reveals her conflicting motives and objectives, as well as her strategic brilliance. Through careful wording, first to the members of her household and then to Potiphar, Potiphar's wife simultaneously condemns and protects Joseph. She also protects herself while removing her nemesis. She begins by making it absolutely clear to the members of her household that Potiphar is to blame for the events. Potiphar, she tells the household, *brought* this Hebrew man to *us*. This deflects blame from Joseph, who should not be held responsible for doing what he was meant to do. Potiphar brought Joseph into his home to mock the members of his household. With this description, Potiphar's wife protects Joseph. Her explanation makes it difficult for both ancient and contemporary readers to condemn her. She is a sexually assertive woman who, once thwarted, protects her intended target and shows him some compassion. An ancient reader would condemn her for the

---

30 Pirson describes this as the "most sensible thing for her to do." Pirson, "Twofold Message," 249.

31 Gen 37:2.

32 Lev 20:10; Deut 22:22.

former, but not the latter. A contemporary reader would celebrate her for both.

According to his wife, Potiphar brought Joseph into his home to mock his household. As Pirson notes, the verb "to mock" (צחק) has a range of meanings, including "to make love, have sexual intercourse."[33] Notably, it appears in the other texts already mentioned that echo Genesis 39. In Genesis 19, Lot tells his sons-in-law to flee the city of Sodom before God destroys it. His sons-in-law think he is joking (מצחק) and remain in the city while Lot and his daughters escape. The verb also appears in the wife-sister story in Genesis 26:8 when Abimelech sees Isaac sporting (מצחק) with Rebecca and realizes that they are married. Given Abimelech's inference, the verb likely describes sexual play in this moment. Noting that Potiphar's wife uses the same verb in her accounting of the event to the members of her household and then to Potiphar but does not specify that Joseph asked her to lie with him when she reports the incident to Potiphar, Pirson suggests that "the verb may have different meanings in both accounts of Potiphar's wife" and that "she makes the most of the verb's ambiguity."[34]

It certainly is hard to imagine that Potiphar introduced Joseph into his household to have sex with all of its members. It is also hard to believe that Potiphar intended Joseph to disrespect his whole household. It makes more sense that Potiphar's wife is expressing the outrage she feels that her husband granted a *Hebrew* man so much status in an Egyptian household. As Joseph says, no one has a greater status than he does in Potiphar's house. That is the mockery to which Potiphar's wife refers.

In truth, Potiphar may not have purchased Joseph to rule in his home, but he grants him this power over time and, therefore, should be held accountable. By emphasizing that Joseph mocks *us*, Potiphar's wife indicates that Joseph's status is an affront to the whole household and not just to her, thereby introducing tension between Potiphar and the members of his household. This would make them less likely to have compassion for Potiphar as the wronged husband and less likely to insist that Joseph be killed for

---

33 Pirson, "Twofold Message," 255.
34 Ibid., 256.

his crimes, especially since they did not witness the events.[35] Seen in this way, Potiphar's wife is protecting Joseph and sowing discord in her home, perhaps as retaliation for her husband's neglect.

Despite her effort to protect him, there is no ambiguity about what she accuses Joseph of. He came to have sex with her, and she cried out. Her cries caused him to run away, leaving his clothing behind. Just as she protected Joseph, she now protects herself by mentioning that she cried out, presumably in protest. As Deuteronomy 22:22–25 legislates, adultery is a capital offense for both parties involved unless the man sexually takes a betrothed woman in a field, in which case only the man is killed. The stated rationale is that in a town, a woman could shout (צעקה) and prevent a man from raping her. Since a woman's shouts could not be heard in a field, there would be doubt whether she wanted or she resisted the sex. By reporting that she shouted, Potiphar's wife tells the members of her household that she was an unwilling victim of Joseph's sexual advances. Therefore, just as Joseph cannot be held accountable for the havoc he wreaked on the household, she cannot be held accountable for what in truth she is guilty of.

Potiphar's wife mentions Joseph's abandoned garment presumably as physical evidence to support her narrative and prove that Joseph was in her home. She clearly wants him gone and the garment helps make her case. Garments play an important role throughout the Joseph story. In Genesis 37, Joseph receives a special garment from his father Jacob that his brothers remove, tear, and dip in blood to convince Jacob of Joseph's death. In Genesis 39, Joseph abandons his clothes in Potiphar's house. In Genesis 41, Joseph receives a signet ring and fine garments from Pharaoh keeping with his high status in Pharaoh's court. The narrative sweep of these chapters suggests that Joseph's clothes mark his identity and tell the story of his transformation and shifts in status.

Garments also play a significant role in the story of Judah and Tamar in Genesis 38—a narrative I address in chapter five that, for some readers, seems to interrupt Joseph's story. Although clothing has significance throughout the Joseph narrative, John R. Huddlestun identifies a particular pattern in the ways clothing is used in

---

35 In biblical law, capital crimes require at least two witnesses to convict. See Num 35:30; Deut 17:6; 19:15.

Genesis 37, 38, and 39 that links these chapters. He observes how deception is a common feature in the three chapters and that the removal or loss of clothing is a key element of that deception.

In Genesis 37, "the removal is accomplished in the most forceful manner (37.23) with the brothers stripping their father's favorite of his precious robe."[36] Although Huddlestun recognizes ambiguity in how Joseph's garment comes to be in Potiphar's wife's possession, he suggests that her act "of grabbing the garment implies a forceful removal," which reminds readers "of the shredded clothing of ch. 37."[37] He also notes how, in Genesis 38, "Tamar's trickery begins with the removal of her 'garments of widowhood' and continues with Judah's surrendering his insignia to Tamar."[38]

Huddlestun observes how, in all three narratives, "the turning point is reached in the narrative when the intended target of the deception is asked, or rather forced, to identify (a) specific object(s), insuring the success of the stratagem."[39] Huddlestun notes that although "Potiphar is not asked to identify the garment as that of Joseph," the reader, "who encounters the deception in ch. 39 *after* chs. 37–38 . . . knows the drill only too well" and that "all that is required is the *implication* of recognition, here conveyed through the stated emotional response and subsequent actions of Potiphar (vv. 19–20)."[40]

Huddlestun's observations about the garment motif in Genesis 37, 38, and 39 are convincing and work to link these three chapters and their characters. Huddlestun perceives a particular connection between the characters of Joseph and Judah. Both characters, he observes, are stripped of "symbols of status and authority" and demoted. He also identifies a crucial difference in their stories and characters. Whereas Joseph resists sex, Judah is eager to have sex. Huddlestun concludes that "the reader is inexorably led

---

36 John R. Huddlestun, "Divestiture, Deception, and Demotion: The Garment Motif in Genesis 37–39," *JSOT* 98 (2002): 55.

37 Huddlestun asks, "Did he leave it *whole* in the hands of the frustrated seductress, seeing that he could not otherwise escape her grasp (v. 12), or was she left holding only a *portion* of it? Or, as some rabbinic exegetes suggest, had Joseph removed it voluntarily prior to his 'change of heart' and subsequent flight?" Ibid.

38 Ibid., 56.

39 Ibid., 57.

40 Ibid.

to contrast the two events as a measure of the character of each."[41] By comparison, Joseph fares far better than Judah.

The links between Genesis 38 and 39 invite another comparison. At the end of Genesis 38, Tamar presents Judah with his staff and seal as evidence that proves the paternity of her baby. Similarly, Potiphar's wife presents Joseph's clothes as evidence that she was sexually assaulted by him. Just as Huddlestun contrasts Joseph and Judah, Peter Bekins contrasts Tamar and Potiphar's wife. In his reading, both are seductresses and "trickster characters" who "obtain evidence from their male counterparts as part of their deceptions." Yet whereas "Tamar is ultimately vindicated for her actions," Potiphar's wife "is foiled in her attempt to seduce and then ruin Joseph."[42]

I agree with Huddlestun and Bekins that the garment motif links Genesis 38 and 39 and invites comparisons of their characters. I also agree with Huddleston that the identification of clothing is an important motif in Genesis 37, 38, and 39 that affirms a character's identity. I disagree that the connection between these chapters and characters works to exonerate Joseph and to condemn Potiphar's wife as the villain in the narrative. In keeping with the motif of clothing as a marker of identity, the presentation of Joseph's garment does identify Joseph. Indeed, he was there alone with Potiphar's wife, as the garment testifies. This is not a lie. Notably, the garment itself is not the means of deception as it was for Joseph's brothers in Genesis 37, who manipulate the garment to substantiate a lie. Potiphar's wife deceives through her words and not with the garment. She lies to her household and to her husband by claiming that Joseph sexually propositioned her.

Potiphar's wife wants people to know that Joseph was present. Her intention is to remove Joseph from the household but, hopefully, not to cause him undue harm. Her accusation that Joseph seduced her ensures that he will be removed from the household. Yet as I stated previously, her specific accusation deflects blame from Joseph and herself and holds Potiphar ultimately accountable for the events that occurred. Perhaps Potiphar will recognize his

---

41 Ibid., 61.
42 Peter Bekins, "Tamar and Joseph in Genesis 38 and 39," *JSOT* 40, no. 4 (2016): 392.

culpability—not unlike Judah does in Genesis 38. After all, Potiphar brought Joseph into the house "to mock" the household or, as the verb can imply, to play sexually with its members. If mockery or sexual play was Potiphar's intent, Joseph cannot be held responsible for fulfilling that intent.

Potiphar's wife's protection of Joseph enables him to continue his narrative journey and fulfill his destiny in Israel's history. Seen in this way, she functions similarly to Tamar in Genesis 38. Like Tamar, Potiphar's wife initiates a prohibited sexual encounter with a man. Tamar is successful. Potiphar's wife is not. Both enable the men in their narratives to fulfill their destiny within Israel's history. Both use clothing to identify their sexual partners and to protect themselves. In my equivocal reading of their stories, neither should be condemned for ensuring the intended and significant narrative outcome. Tamar secures the Davidic monarchy by providing Judah with an heir. Potiphar's wife enables Joseph to continue his journey so that he can begin his rise in Pharaoh's court.

Potiphar's wife provides her husband with a slightly altered account of the events in Genesis 39:16–18:

> She left his garment beside her until his master came to his house. She relayed these things saying: "The Hebrew slave which you brought to us to play with me. When I raised my voice and cried out, he abandoned his garment with me and fled outside."

This passage emphasizes the master-servant relationship first by referring to Potiphar as *his master* and Joseph as *the Hebrew slave*. The emphasis suggests that the crime committed is primarily a social and not a sexual violation. Joseph, a Hebrew slave, is guilty of overstepping boundaries. She continues to hold Potiphar responsible for bringing Joseph into the household, although she implies that Joseph was intended specifically for her. In her account to her husband, she does not include the detail that Joseph came to lie with her. This missing detail may support Pirson's suggestion that Joseph was purchased to sleep with Potiphar's wife, making the inclusion of this detail unnecessary.

In Pirson's reading, Joseph flees once Potiphar's wife screams, whether from pleasure or protest, because "Joseph did not want to be caught in bed with his master's wife" and, therefore, "takes an action similar to Onan's in Genesis 38: *coitus interruptus*."[43] Pirson further posits that Potiphar's wife displays the garment to Potiphar to prove "the great lengths she had—unsuccessfully—gone to."[44] She had tried to have sex with Joseph as was intended, but he did not fulfill his duty. Not only is she innocent of wrongdoing; she should be commended for trying to fulfill Potiphar's intentions. Pirson's reading helps explain the story's conclusion in Genesis 39:19–20:

> When his master heard the words his wife reported to him saying: "These things your servant did to me," he became angry. Joseph's master took him and placed him in the house of confinement, the place where the king's prisoners were kept. He was in the house of confinement.

The passage also emphasizes the servant-master relationship, suggesting that Joseph is guilty of disobedience and not adultery. As I mentioned, adultery is a capital offense. If Potiphar believed that Joseph was guilty of adultery, he would demand the death penalty, not imprisonment, as a punishment. Pirson suggests that Joseph is not imprisoned but reassigned to work in Pharaoh's prison.

According to Pirson, Potiphar is angry because Joseph does not do what he was supposed to do by refusing to sleep with Potiphar's wife. As a result, Potiphar "employs him somewhere else."[45] McKay similarly observes that Joseph "has gained a new position that leads to advancement."[46] McKay further notes how Potiphar's wife "has neither gained nor lost position or status" at the narrative's equivocal conclusion and how Joseph's "innocence is never established,

---

43 Pirson, "Twofold Message," 257.

44 Ibid., 258.

45 Ibid. Pirson concludes, "This is why Potiphar cannot keep Joseph in his household any longer: the attractive and good-looking youth (39,6) did not do the thing he was intended to do, despite the excellent conditions that Potiphar created for him. . . . Therefore Joseph is not stoned to death because of attempted rape, but ends up doing a new job in jail because of his refusal to do that particular thing he was commanded to do, or even bought for to do." Ibid., 259.

46 McKay, "Confronting Redundancy," 228.

but neither is his alleged guilt punished."[47] Joseph "moves onward and upward to the pinnacle role of his career, that of managing Pharaoh, and becomes the most powerful of officials controlling all the food in Egypt."[48]

At the story's conclusion, Joseph is where he was meant to be—a lowly figure in Pharaoh's court. He transitioned from serving as the highest member of Potiphar's house to serving, or being imprisoned, in the lowest segment of Pharaoh's house. Of course, the pattern of his life predicts his rise within Pharaoh's court, as the chapter's conclusion makes clear in Genesis 39:21–23:

> God was with Joseph and extended to him kindness and made the officer of the house of confinement look favorably upon him. The officer of the house of confinement placed all the prisoners in the house of confinement in Joseph's charge, and everything that was done there, he did. The officer of the house of confinement delegated all to him for YHWH was with him. Whatever he did, YHWH made him successful [מצליח].

The story concludes as it began. Joseph is in a lowly state, but God is with him and will grant him success. As he has done before, Joseph falls only to rise again with God's help.

CONCLUSIONS

In my equivocal reading of Genesis 39, Joseph is blessed but not righteous. This distinction is crucial to the Bible's narrative. Joseph succeeds because God is with him and not because he is worthy of success. In fact, he succeeds against all odds. This is the point of Joseph's story. His success, like Israel's, manifests exclusively by God's power and grace. God is the force that directs Joseph's life and Israel's story.

Joseph must be brought low to show how God can elevate the lowly—a Hebrew slave can become second in Potiphar's house and

---

47 Ibid., 229.
48 Ibid.

Pharaoh's court just as an enslaved people can become God's treasured people. Potiphar's wife plays an important role in Joseph's narrative and is instrumental in bringing Joseph down so that God can elevate him. Much like the clothing she presents as evidence, she functions like a narrative device that signals a transition in Joseph's status.

Potiphar's wife may be trouble, but she is not the villain in this story. Fuchs is correct that she is treacherous, but incorrect that she is lethal. An equivocal reading reveals the nuances of her character. She certainly is a woman of desire, and this is unsettling in the biblical context. Yet given that her husband may be a eunuch, her desires could be justified. Whatever their motivation, her desires are not met. No harm is done; no crime committed. Thwarted, Potiphar's wife wants Joseph gone, but she does not want Joseph killed. Her report to her household and husband protects Joseph and herself. Without witnesses, she proves he was present by presenting his clothes. She protects herself by claiming that she cried out. Most importantly, she holds Potiphar ultimately accountable for what happened. He brought Joseph into the household and elevated him, creating domestic chaos. Potiphar's wife acknowledges that there is a force beyond her desires that is guiding events. She suggests that the force is Potiphar, but the reader knows that it is God. Potiphar, his wife, and Joseph are all passive figures directed by God. Joseph comes to understand God's plan and expresses his understanding later when his brothers confront him after their father's death. The brothers fear Joseph will seek vengeance now that Jacob is dead, but Joseph assures them in Genesis 50:19–20, "Don't fear! Am I a substitute for God? Where you intended to harm me, God intended it for good—to make this moment—the survival of many people."

Potiphar's wife and Joseph are equivocal figures with conflicting and suspect motives and characteristics. Their story does not condemn one as the villain or commend the other as the hero. Rather, their story reveals how God directs events in surprising ways. Only God can elevate the lowly. Only God can ensure that an Israelite slave can ascend in an Egyptian home, only to fall and then rise again. Both Joseph and Potiphar's wife are God's instruments. Both enable the story to unfold as it must, to reveal God's power. Theirs is a story of success, not of righteousness. Given this, both must be considered successful in revealing God's providence.

Chapter Two

HANNAH

Hannah's story is deceptively simple. It opens the books of Samuel and Kings that chronicle the Northern and Southern monarchies yet feels more at home among the matriarchal stories found in Genesis. Like the matriarchal narratives, Hannah's story is about becoming a mother. Hannah experiences infertility as did the foremothers Sarah, Rebecca, and Rachel. She must contend with a rival wife who is able to conceive, as Sarah and Rachel did. Ultimately, Hannah conceives and bears a son. Yet Hannah's story takes a unique path in overcoming infertility. By doing so, it defies readers' expectations and reveals complexities in both its narrative and its central character.

In general, equivocal readings disclose complexities in biblical narratives as well as in those who read them. Equivocal readings reveal a depth of character and story that extends beyond convention and enables readers to integrate their generous and suspicious perspectives in the analysis of a text. My equivocal reading of Hannah's story responds to the specific challenges it poses for feminist biblical readers who, despite Hannah's independence and strength, consider her story to be about a woman who wants to produce a son.

When viewed this way, Hannah's story conforms to a biblical pattern of women serving their husbands, as well as the patriarchal values of biblical narratives, by having sons. My equivocal reading recognizes the validity of this interpretation but offers a way to perceive Hannah as a powerful figure whose character and story are defined, but not limited by, her gender. Hannah's story reveals the power she exerts over her own life, the life of her family, and even God.

In my equivocal reading, Hannah embodies and embraces her womanhood. Her story *is* about her desire to become a mother, yet as I show, Hannah does not want a child for her husband. She wants a child for herself. Hannah's willingness to relinquish her young child in service to God reveals that she wants the experience of maternity even more than the child himself.

Hannah's desire to have a child aligns with the premium value the Bible ascribes to fertility and conforms to the Bible's patriarchal ideology, which values women primarily for their contributions to the patriline. Yet to consider this desire to be purely in service of patriarchal interests or concerns, as many feminist readers do, fails to acknowledge the ways maternity is an essential female experience that should be valued.

Feminist Critique of Motherhood in the Bible

The Bible tells many stories about mothers—particularly about women who face challenges to become mothers, such as infertility (matriarchs Sarah, Rebecca, and Rachel) or dead husbands (Tamar in Genesis 38 and Ruth). Esther Fuchs convincingly interprets the common biblical trope of motherhood as serving the Bible's patriarchal interests by "routing the resourcefulness of mothers in the 'proper' direction," which is "the sustenance and perpetuation of the patrilineal continuity."[1]

According to Fuchs, the Bible does not celebrate women for their procreative powers. It does not celebrate the female bodies that birth and nurture babies. Instead, the Bible celebrates women's "initiative in obviating obstacles to patrilineal continuity," such as barrenness.[2] Fuchs views biblical mothers like Sarah, Rebecca,

---

1 Fuchs, *Sexual Politics*, 47.

2 Fuchs writes, "This explains the preponderance of narratives about barren wives, who manage to give birth despite the odds. This also explains the repeated validation of childless women who succeed against the odds in giving birth to a male heir. Such mother-figures are indeed implicitly or explicitly praised not despite but because of the Bible's patriarchal policy." Ibid.

Rachel, and Leah as serving patriarchal interests and not as serving their own personal or biological desires.

Fuchs correctly names an essential element of these mothers' stories—the desire to have a male heir to secure the patriline. Of course, men also desire male heirs. Despite these male desires, Fuchs observes how the Bible's "nativity narratives" focus on women's efforts to overcome fertility obstacles. For Fuchs, this reflects a deeply embedded patriarchal ideology. Fuchs argues that the Bible associates morality with fertility and observes how good women are "rewarded with sons," whereas barrenness reflects a "moral deficiency." Furthermore, she asserts that the repeated motif of barrenness makes infertility an exclusively female problem. Men, observes Fuchs, "are associated with permanent fertility, while in women fertility is a contingency if not a rarity."[3]

J. Cheryl Exum draws similar conclusions to Fuchs's about the biblical depictions of mothers and motherhood. Exum recognizes the power of the Bible's mothers. Yet like Fuchs, Exum suggests that the Bible's depiction of mothers supports a patriarchal social order that ultimately works against female empowerment. Exum argues that the Bible depicts women who strive to overcome infertility "as mean-spirited, deceptive, and untrustworthy—and for these reasons, a threat to the patriarchal social order."[4] These "dangerous" women, according to Exum, "must be kept in their place, the mother's place, the place for the other where patriarchy can control them."[5]

I begin with this feminist critique of the Bible's mothers because I find it convincing and challenging. As a feminist reader, I am suspicious of how a male-centric text like the Bible depicts its women, particularly when it co-opts female experiences like maternity and centers women's lives and narratives on these experiences in a reductionist way. It is hard to find biblical female characters whose stories are not defined by motherhood. Fuchs also keenly observes how the Bible loses interest in its mothers once the heir is born and his legacy is secured.[6]

---

3 Ibid., 49.

4 J. Cheryl Exum, *Fragmented Women: Feminist (Sub)versions of Biblical Narratives* (Valley Forge, PA: Trinity International, 1993), 135–36.

5 Ibid., 136.

6 Fuchs, *Sexual Politics*, 46.

This critique is particularly challenging to me and to readers who search for narrative elements that stand apart from, or in tension with, the Bible's overarching patriarchal ideology. In the main, I agree with Fuchs and Exum. The Bible reflects a patriarchal ideology that considers women to be threatening. Its stories often expose and work to contain that threat.[7] Yet as a religious-critical reader, I seek to offset my suspicious reading with a generous one and am not content with the feminist critique of biblical mothers. I want maternal power to serve more than the patriarchal agenda and biblical mothers to manifest more than patriarchal interests. As a woman, I recognize, experience, and celebrate maternal power. As a religious woman, I view maternal power as being aligned with divine power. My equivocal perspective, I argue, allows me to see how Hannah's story recognizes maternal power independent of its patriarchal agenda and aligns it with divine power.

I perceive maternity to be an essential female experience and relish the significant role a biblical mother has while understanding that she seeks heirs for her husband's patriline. I agree with Fuchs and Exum that biblical stories about mothers reflect a social dynamic that privileges men and a religious dynamic that showcases God's power by demonstrating that God opens wombs and controls fertility.[8] Maternal power in the Bible must be read within the context of this male- and God-privileging ideology, but it also must be recognized.[9] Simply put, mothers are powerful and central figures in the Bible.

I value the expression of female power in the Bible and am unwilling to flatten any of the Bible's female characters by seeing them purely as instruments of a male-privileging ideology. Let me be clear: I am not a naive reader. I fully understand that biblical

---

7 This is the general argument of my work on sisters and sisterhoods in the Bible. See Amy Kalmanofsky, *Dangerous Sisters of the Hebrew Bible* (Minneapolis: Fortress, 2014).

8 Gen 21:1–2; 25:21; 29:31; 30:22; 1 Sam 1:19.

9 It is important to note that a God-privileging ideology is also male-privileging since the Bible's God is gendered male; as Fuchs writes, "According to this system, man is a more 'authentic' representative of God because God is male, and God is male because the Bible reflects a masculine construction of the divine." Fuchs, *Sexual Politics*, 12. See also my discussion of God's gender in Kalmanofsky, *Gender-Play*, 9–11.

women, most likely, are a construct of elite men who embody and promote a male-privileging ideology.[10] These men may seek to control and limit female power, but at least, I argue, they perceived it, which suggests they experienced it. Also, I argue that just because an essentially female experience like maternity is portrayed by male authors does not mean there is nothing true to a woman's experience in its depiction or nothing of value to be drawn from it.

Biblical maternal narratives certainly showcase God's power, but they often do so by depicting strong women and surprisingly weak men. Sarah is the dominating force in her maternal narrative, which culminates in God commanding Abraham to obey Sarah as she secures her son Isaac's position as heir in Genesis 21. In Genesis 30, the competing mothers Rachel and Leah trade mandrakes for having sex with Jacob in order to have more babies. Elkanah, in Hannah's narrative, and Manoah, in the Samson narrative in Judges 13, are essentially absent fathers whose wives engage with divine beings that ensure their fertility.

The Bible's willingness to depict strong women—even if in service of the patriarchal plot, as Fuchs and Exum suggest—is noteworthy. It is also important to note that maternal strength is manifest in a variety of ways. Biblical mothers are strong in body and spirit. We see them plot, withstand ridicule and pain, and struggle with rivals to have and protect their children. Their stories reflect the value of fertility and the Bible's investment in patrilineal descent, but they also attest to a fuller range of a woman's experience than simply the desire to have children to continue her husband's line.

Producing a male heir is one reason but not the only reason why biblical women want children.[11] To not recognize these other

---

10 Most scholars assume that elite men were the Bible's authors. Carol Meyers observes, "The male gender of the authors and editors of the Hebrew Bible is not the only problem, and it may not be the major one. Their *social position* is also a serious factor. Most of the male authors and editors were part of a literary elite, a tiny and unrepresentative minority." Carol Meyers, *Rediscovering Eve: Ancient Israelite Women in Context* (Oxford: Oxford University Press, 2013), 18. It is possible that women authors did contribute to the Bible. See S. D. Goitein, "Women as Creators of Biblical Genres," *Prooftexts* 8, no. 1 (1988): 1–33.

11 Rachel's jealousy of her sister Leah motivates her to have a child (Gen 30:1). Leah's desire for Jacob motivates her, as the names of her first three children indicate (Gen 29:32–34). See my discussion in Kalmanofsky, *Dangerous Sisters*, 25. There are even women who do not seem to want children, despite the value of having a male heir.

elements is to diminish these women and their stories. As we see in Hannah's story, biblical women also have children to satisfy their own needs apart from their husbands' desires. Their stories and characters are open to more meaning and nuance than the feminist critique of the maternal narrative allows.

An Equivocal Reading of 1 Samuel 1: Hannah's Demand

Generations of readers consider the character of Hannah as significant. The rabbis glean proper behaviors and attitudes for praying from Hannah's story.[12] Feminist biblical scholars assess Hannah's strength and the agency she wields over her fate.[13] Most readers, whether ancient or contemporary, concur that Hannah is a remarkable figure in the biblical context. Unable to have a child and saddled with a husband who does not seem to care enough to help her, Hannah works alone to overturn her infertility and appeals directly to God. She does not rely on a husband or a handmaiden. In response to Hannah's appeal (if not demand), God enables Hannah to bear the prophet Samuel, who anoints Israel's first king, Saul.

Hannah's desire to have a child does not make her a remarkable figure in the Bible. This desire alone would make Hannah, as Fuchs sees her, a typical "pious woman who trusts that Yhwh will redeem her from barrenness," who serves solely as a pawn in the patriarchal plot.[14] Rather, it is the means with which she obtains her child and

---

The Shunammite in 2 Kgs 4 and Manoah's wife in Judg 13 do not ask for children. Miriam is unmarried and childless, suggesting that there can be more to a woman's story than marriage and fertility.

12 B. Berakhot 31A.

13 For example, see Lillian R. Klein, "Hannah: Marginalized Victim and Social Redeemer," in *A Feminist Companion to Samuel and Kings*, ed. Athalya Brenner (Sheffield, UK: Sheffield Academic, 1994), 77–92; and Carol Meyers, "Hannah and Her Sacrifice: Reclaiming Female Agency," in Brenner, *Feminist Companion*, 93–104. Meyers concludes her analysis, "A woman's visibility and centrality in the Hannah Narrative of 1 Samuel 1 and her agency in a ritual act thus reveal an otherwise hidden aspect of women's cultic life. In addition, Hannah's sacrifice signifies an instance of female activity—albeit related to maternal functions—with national implications. By the very individuality of her characterization and behavior, she is represented as contributing to the corporate welfare of ancient Israel." Ibid., 104.

14 Fuchs, *Sexual Politics*, 59.

the power she asserts over the men in her life that make Hannah a remarkable figure.

Hannah's agency and influence are apparent even in her relationship with God. As the ultimate power in any biblical narrative, God grants Hannah's request and gifts her with a child. Yet at the end of the story, Hannah gifts the child back to God, demonstrating that Hannah has the ability to ask of and be answered by God as well as the ability to give to God. Hannah meets her own emotional needs by having this child, but her gift suggests that the child serves God's needs as well and that Hannah can provide for God. Hannah's story begins in 1 Samuel 1:1–3:

> There was a man from Ramathaim-zophim, from the hill country of Ephraim whose name was Elkanah son of Jeroham son of Elihu son of Tohu son of Zuph, the Ephratite. He had two wives. The first named Hannah, the second Peninnah. Peninnah had children, but Hannah had no children. This man would go up yearly from his city to worship and to offer sacrifices to YHWH of Hosts in Shiloh where the two sons of Eli, Hophni and Phinehas, were priests of YHWH.

Readers familiar with the ancestor stories from Genesis can anticipate what happens next. Two wives—one of whom is barren—suggest a fertility showdown similar to the ones between Sarah and Hagar and Rachel and Leah. Infertility is overturned, and a blessed child and heir is born.

Elkanah's name, which means God creates or God acquires, makes clear God's role in the production of this expected new life. Elkanah's role is less clear. Hopeful fathers like Abraham in Genesis 15 and Isaac in Genesis 25:21 appeal to God for children. Elkanah does not appeal to God on Hannah's behalf, but not for lack of opportunity. He makes a yearly pilgrimage to the shrine at Shiloh and easily could have prayed there for Hannah to conceive. Instead, in 1 Samuel 1:4–6 we read that he offers sacrifices and apportions shares to his wives and children:

> One day, Elkanah offered a sacrifice. He gave portions to Peninnah his wife and to all her sons and daughters. But to Hannah he gave one portion even though [אפס כי] he

43

loved Hannah, though YHWH had closed her womb. Her rival agitated her to trembling because God had closed her womb.

The phrase אפים כי is difficult. My translation assumes the intended phrase was אף ספכי, which communicates that Hannah did not receive preferential treatment from Elkanah "even though" he loved her.[15]

Elkanah appears unconcerned by Hannah's lack of children, which plays with readers' expectations of what infertility in the Bible typically triggers. He does not pray on Hannah's behalf, nor does he compensate her. He does not invite God into the narrative as Isaac does in Genesis 25:21, nor does he do something to spur rivalry between the women as Jacob does by clearly preferring one wife over the other (Gen 29:30). Elkanah loves Hannah, but he may not love her more than Peninnah. Whether jealous or not, Peninnah knows that she has an advantage over Hannah and taunts her for her infertility.

The phrase "God had closed her womb" appears twice in this passage, making clear that Hannah's infertility is an act of divine intervention. God's role in Hannah's barrenness could indicate a character or moral deficiency, as Fuchs suggests.[16] It also could be an invitation to engage with God, thereby propelling the narrative forward. In the Bible, women most often engage with God around becoming or being mothers, as Fuchs observes, "Procreative contexts are the only ones in which women address Yhwh and hold a dialogue with him. Yhwh either responds to the actions of mother-figures, or sends emissaries to them. As mothers, women are most often shown to act in accordance with a broader divine plan."[17] As I noted previously, Fuchs views this as an essential part of the patriarchal strategy that serves male interests. Yet it is possible to offer a more generous reading, in which the desire for and experience of

---

15 Other translations of this difficult phrase suggest that Hannah does receive preferential treatment. See Hans Wilhelm Hertzberg, *I & II Samuel*, trans. J. S. Bowden (Philadelphia: Westminster, 1964), 24.

16 This is Fuchs's general assumption about infertile women. There is no textual evidence for Hannah's moral deficiency that would justify her infertility. Also, Fuchs admits that "Hannah stands out as an exceptionally pious woman who trusts that Yhwh will redeem her from barrenness." Fuchs, *Sexual Politics*, 59.

17 Ibid., 45.

maternity provide a natural and logical opportunity for a woman to engage with God. In fact, maternity may provide the greatest opportunity in human experience for intimacy with God.[18]

In the Bible, God is invested in all kinds of fertility—human, animal, and agricultural.[19] Given this, a woman's desire for fertility aligns her directly with God's central desire. I argue that fertility is valued, and pregnancy desired, in the Bible not to subjugate women and to amplify male power—although this may be a by-product—but because life is valued to sustain Israelite society.[20] This emphasis on life may reflect the very practical needs of ancient Israel's small-subsistence farming economy that depended on a human workforce, and the emphasis may work to support a patriarchal agenda. But a generous reading perceives the positive aspects

18 Rachel E. Adelman suggests that during pregnancy, a woman shares intimate knowledge with God, and she comments on Rebecca's difficult pregnancy, "What sets Rebekah apart from Isaac is her insight into the discrepancy between the outer norms (the election of the firstborn) and the inner truth of the divine plan. She also exemplifies the difficulty in externalizing that inner, divine truth as embodied in her intimate, womb-bound knowledge found in the tumult within her belly." Rachel E. Adelman, *The Female Ruse: Women's Deception and Divine Sanction in the Hebrew Bible* (Sheffield, UK: Sheffield Phoenix, 2015), 21.

19 Tikva Frymer-Kensky comments on agricultural fertility, "Like the other Near Eastern peoples, Israel was concerned with fertility. In order to feel secure on the land, the people must be assured of God's power to ensure fertility. However, the biblical understanding of fertility is radically different from that of ancient Near Eastern polytheism. Israelite prayer and ritual cannot facilitate the union of the forces of the cosmos; only the worship of one God is allowed. Therefore, God alone must unite all the forces that produce fertility. God must be the only power who brings fertility, and God alone must be enough." Tikva Frymer-Kensky, *In the Wake of the Goddesses: Women, Culture, and the Biblical Transformation of Pagan Myth* (New York: Free Press, 1992), 92. Commenting on human fertility, Frymer-Kensky writes, "God oversees the entire process of gestation and childbirth: God forms and shapes the child in the womb, God takes note of the child in the womb, cares for it there, and may call the child into service there; God is midwife, bringing on the labor and bringing forth the child. . . . God, the master of all the other elements of the natural world, is master of human reproduction as well." Ibid., 98.

20 Women needed to have children in order to produce the workforce necessary to sustain life in ancient Israel, as Carol Meyers observes, "Productive labor is, in a sense, a demographic issue that affects family size and gender roles. For the Israelites, the hard work of both women and men and the reproductive capacity of women were the necessary responses to considerable labor needs." Meyers, *Rediscovering Eve*, 50.

of emphasizing fertility. Pregnancy not only provides a woman with an opportunity for intimacy with God but also provides an opportunity to align, and perhaps even identify, with God. Several biblical passages use maternal imagery to describe God.[21] It would be reasonable to assume that the use of this imagery validates women's experiences and creates an opportunity for a woman to see herself and her experience aligned with God's self and experience.

Not only does Elkanah appear unbothered by Hannah's infertility, but he also appears unconcerned with Peninnah's taunting Hannah, assuming he witnessed it. In contrast, Hannah reacts strongly in 1 Samuel 1:7–8:

> This happened every year. When she would go up to the house of YHWH, she [Peninnah] would agitate her [Hannah] so that she wept and did not eat. Elkanah, her husband, said to her: "Hannah, why are you weeping? Why are you not eating? Why are you so sad? Am I not better for you than ten sons?"

Elkanah understands Hannah's refusal to participate in the communal meal that accompanied the sacrifice as a sign of her despair. He assumes that Hannah is more upset by her infertility than by Peninnah's taunts. Although attuned somewhat to her emotional life, Elkanah is incredulous that Hannah could be that upset. After all, she may not have children, but she has Elkanah.

In my reading of this passage, Elkanah appears at his best as clueless. Elkanah misreads the situation and focuses only on himself. He also misperceives Hannah's reaction as purely emotional. Hannah's weeping and fasting are more than emotional reactions to her situation. They are strategies she employs to address her situation. With an unresponsive husband, Hannah takes control of her

---

21 See Isa 42:14; 46:3–4; 49:14–15; 66:12–14; Jer 31:20. For discussions of God as mother, see Julia A. Foster, "The Motherhood of God: The Use of *ḥyl* as God-Language in the Hebrew Scriptures," in *Uncovering Ancient Stones: Essays in Memory of H. Neil Richardson*, ed. Lewis M. Hopfe (Winona Lake, IN: Eisenbrauns, 1994), 93–102; Marc Zvi Brettler, "Incompatible Metaphors for YHWH in Isaiah 40–66," *JSOT* 78 (1998): 97–120; and Phyllis Trible, "The Gift of a Poem: A Rhetorical Study of Jeremiah 31:15–22," *Andover Newton Quarterly* 17, no. 4 (1977): 271–80.

fate. Weeping and fasting are ritual acts in the Bible.[22] Weeping is a ritual act associated particularly with women, as Jeremiah 9:16–20 illustrates. This passage describes professional female lamenters who weep and wail in mourning. Both ritual acts are intended to capture God's attention. In 2 Samuel 12:16–23, King David fasts and weeps in an effort to save his dying son. He stops fasting and weeping once the child dies, and his efforts prove fruitless. Similarly, Daughter Zion's weeping in the book of Lamentations could be viewed as a prayerful act designed to get God's attention.[23] In Lamentations, Zion's tears bear witness to her suffering.[24] She wants God to see her anguish and respond.[25]

Lacking her husband's concern or assistance, Hannah employs strategies at her disposal to appeal to God on her own behalf. She weeps and fasts. She also prays and vows in 1 Samuel 1:9–11,

> After the eating and drinking at Shiloh, Hannah got up. The priest Eli was sitting on the seat by the doorpost of the temple of YHWH. She was bitter of spirit when she prayed to YHWH and wept. She vowed a vow and said: "YHWH of Hosts, if you look upon the suffering of your maidservant and remember me and not forget your maidservant, and if you give your maidservant seed of humans, I will give him to YHWH all the days of his life, and no razor shall touch his head."

At this moment, Hannah takes complete charge of her situation and uses all the tools available to her as a woman to appeal to God,

---

22 See David Lambert, "Fasting as a Penitential Rite: A Biblical Phenomenon?," *Harvard Theological Review* 96, no. 4 (2003): 477–512.

23 In this way, Daughter Zion functions like the weeping goddess figure found throughout Mesopotamian lament literature. See F. W. Dobbs-Allsopp, *Weep, O Daughter Zion: A Study of the City-Lament Genre in the Hebrew Bible*, BibOr 44 (Rome: Pontifical Biblical Institute, 1993); Samuel Noah Kramer, "Weeping Goddess: Sumerian Prototypes of the *Mater Dolorosa*," *BA* 46 (1983): 69–79; and Amy Kalmanofsky, "Their Heart Cried Out to God: Gender and Prayer in the Book of Lamentations," in *A Question of Sex? Gender and Difference in the Hebrew Bible and Beyond*, ed. Deborah W. Rooke (Sheffield, UK: Sheffield Phoenix, 2007), 53–65.

24 The figure of Daughter Zion weeps often in Lamentations. See Lam 1:2, 16; 2:11, 18.

25 This is my argument in Kalmanofsky, "Their Heart Cried Out," 53–65.

to address God directly, and even to manipulate God into meeting her demands.

Her tears, fasting, and prayers are powerful ways to communicate her distress and to attract God's concern. Yet her vow may be the strongest means she employs. Numbers 30 presents the laws related to vows. Vows establish an if-then situation that enables humans to set conditions upon God. For example, when Jacob travels in Mesopotamia, he vows in Genesis 28:20–22 that if God protects and sustains him through his journey and returns him to his father's house, then Jacob will accept YHWH to be his god. Men and women can vow, although a woman's vow could be annulled by her father or her husband. Elkanah could overturn Hannah's vow. It is unclear at this point if he is aware of Hannah's vow. The priest Eli appears to be the only possible witness to Hannah's vow.

In her vow, Hannah asks specifically for the seed of humans.[26] Many translations assume she wants a son and translate the phrase as "male child" (e.g., NJPSV), which supports Fuchs's claim that the birth of a male heir is the "telos of all biblical nativity scenes."[27] Given the value of having a male heir in the Bible, this assumption makes sense. Yet the text does not make this clear. The use of the strange phrase "seed of humans" leaves open the possibility that Hannah was invested in having a child—whether male or female. The fact that the child assumes Nazirite behaviors and does not have its hair cut also does not clarify its gender. According to Numbers 6:2, males and females could become Nazirites. I suggest that the phrase "seed of humans" does not clarify the gender of the child and intentionally leaves vague who the father is. Hannah does not ask for a son of Elkanah and seems willing to accept any man's seed. Of course, Hannah does have a male child, the prophet Samuel, and so her efforts to secure this child affirm the assumptions that biblical mothers serve the patriarchal interests of their narratives by wanting and having male heirs.

Yet my reading suggests that Hannah was not necessarily invested in a male child. Rather, Hannah wanted to have a child, and doing so serves her own needs and desires. She is the only

---

26 The exact translation of the unique phrase זרע אנשים is "seed of men" or "human seed" and not "male seed."

27 Fuchs, *Sexual Politics*, 47.

one who wants her to have a child—whether to become a mother or to stop Peninnah from tormenting her. Either way, she is self-motivated and proactively works on her own behalf. This reading empowers Hannah. It also elevates the female experience without seeing it as being in service of male needs. Hannah wants to have a child for no one's benefit in her family but her own. She wants to be a mother. This child, this seed of humans—of any man—will not benefit Elkanah's home or patriline. The child will not be given to Elkanah. In fulfillment of Hannah's vow, the child will be given to God for "all the days of his life."

Elkanah is not the only man to misread Hannah's emotional reality. Eli does as well when he responds to Hannah's prayer in 1 Samuel 1:12–17:

> As she continued to pray before YHWH, Eli watched her mouth. Hannah was speaking in her heart; only her lips moved, but her voice was not heard. Eli thought she was drunk. Eli said to her: "How long will you be drunk? Remove your wine from upon you!" Hannah responded and said: "No, my lord, I am a bitter woman. Wine and strong drink I have not drunk. Rather, I pour out my soul before YHWH. Do not think of your maidservant as worthless. Rather it is from my great distress and upset that I speak." Eli responded and said: "Go in peace. May the God of Israel grant your request which you ask of him."

Eli misreads Hannah's fervor as drunkenness and does not appear to register her misery. This may discredit Eli. Yet Eli is easily corrected and accepts Hannah's piety. It is interesting that without knowing what Hannah prays for, Eli expresses the desire that God grant Hannah her request. Perhaps Eli assumes that a woman would pray this fervently only for a child and, therefore, affirms Hannah's desire.

HANNAH'S GIFT

Eli also may be asserting his authority at this moment, suggesting that his approval of Hannah's prayer is necessary for God to respond. In verse 18, Hannah certainly appears relieved when she leaves Eli's presence and now can eat. Yet 1 Samuel 1:19–20 makes it clear that God responds to Hannah's prayer and not to Eli's request on her behalf:

> They arose early in the morning to worship before YHWH and returned to their home in Ramah. Elkanah knew his wife Hannah and YHWH remembered Hannah. In time, Hannah conceived and gave birth to a son. She named him Samuel because from YHWH I requested him.

God remembers Hannah and gives her a son. Hannah understands that God answered *her* prayer and names the child Samuel.

Readers note how the etymology of Samuel's name (כי מיהוה שאלתיו) fits better the character of Saul (שאול). Some scholars suggest that elements of Saul's birth narrative were "transferred to Samuel."[28] Whether their birth stories in fact are intertwined, it is true that the characters of Saul and Samuel appear literarily connected through the full course of their narratives, as I discuss in the next chapter. Hannah evokes Saul when she names Samuel and, in this way, effectively births both characters into the narrative.

Elkanah has no role besides providing the male seed that produces the child. He does not name or bless the child. Instead, he goes about his routine and cedes the decisions around the care of the child to Hannah in 1 Samuel 1:21–23:

> Elkanah went up, along with his household, to offer a yearly sacrifice to YHWH and his votive sacrifice. But Hannah did not go up for she said to her husband: "When the child is weaned, I will bring him. And he will appear before YHWH and stay there forever." Elkanah her husband said to her: "Do what is right in your eyes. Stay until you wean him. May YHWH establish his word." The woman remained and nursed her son until she weaned him.

Hannah's delay in fulfilling her vow is notable and supports my reading that Hannah's desire to experience motherhood motivates

---

28 See P. Kyle McCarter Jr., *I Samuel: A New Translation*, Anchor Bible 8 (New York: Doubleday, 1980), 65.

her more than the desire to have a male heir or to respond to Peninnah's taunts. Hannah wants to keep her child with her as long as possible and does not seem to care about or be aware of Elkanah's benefit or desire. As I mentioned, this child will live forever in God's house and not in Elkanah's. Hannah prolongs her own relationship with the child, not Elkanah's. Also, Hannah appears to bear no lasting grudge against or concern for Peninnah. Peninnah plays no part in the story going forward and is not even mentioned once Hannah prays for a child. Hannah's desire to keep the child with her until he is weaned suggests that she wants to experience motherhood as long as possible. She does this for herself. She wants to nourish and care for the child before relinquishing him into God's care. Hannah's desire to mother Samuel remains evident after she brings him to God. First Samuel 2:19 describes how Hannah makes a coat for Samuel and brings it to him each year in the temple.

Again, it is possible to view Hannah's desire to be a mother—to nurse and nurture a child—as a biologically determined reality that limits female experience to being in service of the patriarchy. Lillian R. Klein observes that Hannah's function as a mother is limited to "reproduction and nursing, the biologically programmed aspects of being female."[29] Interestingly, Klein does not note Hannah's yearly gift of a coat that enables her to continue to mother Samuel. Also, Klein does not acknowledge the elements in the "biologically programmed aspects" that may have given Hannah great emotional satisfaction, if not joy. My reading challenges Klein's assumptions. Earlier I suggested that Hannah wants a child, and not specifically a son. I also think that mothering for Hannah means more than what biology demands. Her body does not demand that she make a coat for Samuel each year. She does this, presumably, to maintain a nurturing relationship with him—to continue to mother him.

Most of all, my reading does not view motherhood as something that limits women's experience, but rather as something integral to it that should be desired and celebrated, not seen only as being in service to a patriarchal ideology. Hannah wants to be a mother separate from Elkanah's needs and desires. She wants to be a mother—to experience motherhood with all of its biological and emotional demands—for herself. But Klein is right to note that

---

29 Klein, "Social Redeemer," 92.

Hannah willingly relinquishes the joys of parenthood. She experiences as much of motherhood as she can before she must fulfill her vow and bring Samuel to God. Her fulfillment of the vow is presented as a sacrifice in 1 Samuel 1:24:

> She brings him up [ותעלהו עמה] with her when she weaned him with three bulls, one ephah of flour, and one skin of wine. She brought the young boy to the house of YHWH at Shiloh.

As Carol Meyers observes, Hannah brings her own animal sacrifice, which should be viewed as "an example of women's religion as it existed at some point early in the history of Israel."[30] Hannah offers this sacrifice in fulfillment of her vow and does not need her husband to offer it on her behalf.[31] Indeed, Hannah brings animals, flour, and wine as an offering, but she also brings her son.

The expression "she brings him up" (ותעלהו) evokes two other biblical passages related to child sacrifice. God commands Abraham to bring his son Isaac up to be sacrificed in Genesis 22:2 (והעלהו שם לעלה). In Judges 11:31, Jephthah vows to offer up to YHWH (העליתהו לעולה) the first thing that comes out from his house to greet him when he returns from battle. Unfortunately, his daughter is the first living being to greet him. Like Abraham and Jephthah, Hannah sacrifices a child. For Abraham and Jephthah, the sacrifice is a matter of life or death. Luckily, Abraham is not made to kill his child. Jephthah must. In contrast to these fathers' sacrifices, Hannah's is not a matter of life or death. But it is a sacrifice nonetheless. All three parents are willing to give up their children to God. The shared phrasing captures how the child leaves the parent's realm for the divine and conveys the magnitude of each moment. It also aligns Hannah with these figures and invites comparison.

Hannah's sacrifice is in response to a vow, like Jephthah's, yet her child, like Abraham's, lives to serve a crucial role in Israel's story. Her story, like Abraham's, shows how God "gives life"; Jephthah's story shows how God "grants death."[32] Given this

---

30 Meyers, "Hannah and Her Sacrifice," 101.
31 Ibid., 102.
32 In her prayer in 1 Samuel 2:6, Hannah praises God who gives life and grants death.

outcome, Hannah appears to be aligned more closely with Abraham. Ritual sacrifices are human offerings to God. The religious and psychological dynamics of sacrifice are complex. It is unclear who is serving whom. Do the sacrifices benefit God and satisfy God's needs? Or do the sacrifices benefit human beings by securing divine favor?[33] The conclusion of Hannah's narrative in 1 Samuel 1:25–28 reveals this complex dynamic while making it clear that Hannah understands that she provides for God:

> They slaughtered the bull and brought the child to Eli. She said: "Please, my lord, as you live my lord, I am the woman who stood before you to pray to YHWH. I prayed for this child and God granted me my request [שאלתי] which I asked from him [שאלתי מעמו]. Indeed, I am giving him [השאלתהו] back to YHWH. For all of his days, he is dedicated [שאול] to YHWH." They worshipped there to YHWH.

The passage plays with the root שאל, which means "to request/ask/demand." In its causative form, it means "to grant a request / to allow someone to make a request / to lend." At first, Hannah admits that she asked God for this child and that God responded to her request. Her statement indicates that she is at God's mercy and that God has the power in their relationship. Interestingly, it does not grant Eli any power or role in what transpires. Eli's hope, expressed in verse 17, that Hannah's prayer be answered had no effect. God responded to Hannah and not to Eli.

In the second part of the statement, the power dynamic shifts. Hannah goes from the one who asks to the one who provides—from שאלתי to השאלתהו. The child she asked for is now the child she gives. He is loaned to God (שאול ליהוה). God did not ask for this child to be born. Hannah's desire for a child and her piety triggered God's response. God responds to Hannah's request for a child just as God responds to the people's request for a king in 1 Samuel 8. Seen in this way, neither Samuel nor Saul was part of God's design. Both are figures born from human needs and desires.

---

33 For an excellent analysis of the symbolism and meaning of the sacrificial cult, see Jonathan Klawans, *Purity, Sacrifice and the Temple: Symbolism and Supersessionism in the Study of Ancient Judaism* (Oxford: Oxford University Press, 2006).

Just as God gives King Saul to Israel, God gives Samuel to Hannah in response to her needs. The child belongs fully to her. She only lends him in service to God.

CONCLUSIONS

Hannah's story can be understood as a triumph of the patriarchy. In this suspicious reading, the focus is on the birth of a son who changes the course of Israel's history. Hannah's story also could be understood as the triumph of a woman who subverts the patriarchy. In this generous reading, the focus is on Hannah and the extraordinary measures she took to become pregnant and to experience motherhood.

My equivocal reading attempts to move beyond the critique offered by some feminist biblical scholars who perceive maternity as being solely in service of a patriarchal ideology. I agree with these scholars that having a baby, particularly a son, serves the Bible's overarching narrative concerns and its implicit patriarchal ideology, but I do not want to limit our understanding of the role of maternity and the narratives about the Bible's mothers to this reading. My reading of Hannah's story argues for viewing maternity as an essential female experience that a woman wants for herself and that aligns her with divine will and presence.

In my introduction, I describe equivocal readings as flexible readings that admit bias and that tolerate discord. As an equivocal reader, I must acknowledge that my positive assessment of Hannah's maternity may be a product of my own desires to see her this way and to view her not simply as a patriarchal pawn. I admit to being predisposed to a generous reading of her story, perhaps because, as a religious-critical reader, I am invested in seeing how the Bible recognizes and celebrates women's power instead of channeling it solely in the service of patriarchal interests. I also may be drawn to a generous reading because my own experience with maternity has shaped my reading of Hannah's story. I have experienced firsthand the complexities of maternity and have felt the ways in which my own needs and desires related to motherhood align or conflict with society's needs and desires. I experienced the biological, societal, and emotional imperatives of motherhood that

I assume are timeless and, therefore, are manifest in the biblical maternal narratives.

My desire to be generous toward maternal narratives may shape the reading I offer, but I argue that Hannah's story is open to this. In an equivocal reading, the generous reading coexists with the suspicious reading. Maternity can restrict and enhance a woman's life and story. A woman like Hannah can serve the Bible's patriarchal agenda while serving her own needs and desires. Hannah may need God to conceive her child, but she can take control of her fate and secure God's assistance. Hannah can ask, and she can demand. She can receive and she can lend.

CHAPTER THREE

SAUL, SAMUEL, HANNAH, AND THE WOMAN FROM EN-DOR

An equivocal reading of a biblical text embraces the complexities of both the characters and the narrative, perceiving character flaws along with heroic acts and recognizing the shifting values that shape a story's construction and reception. As we saw in chapter one, complexity can be revealed through intertextual readings that identify verbal echoes between narratives across biblical chapters and books. These echoes add literary dimensions to the connected narratives as well as provide a broader biblical perspective.

In this chapter, through an equivocal reading of 1 Samuel 28, we see how complexity also reveals itself through a network of relationships intentionally formed among characters. We see how King Saul, the prophet Samuel, the medium from En-dor, and Hannah form a literary network that works to tell a complex narrative about a complex figure.

King Saul is among the most complicated figures in the Bible. There is much to like about him and much to dislike. Rising from obscurity to prominence, he reluctantly becomes Israel's first king and then reluctantly loses the throne and dies an ignoble death. There are two accounts of Saul's death. In battle against the Philistines, Saul either falls on his own sword (1 Sam 31) or is killed by a rogue Amalekite (2 Sam 1). His body is stripped, beheaded, and impaled. Despite Saul's brutal death and the maltreatment of his body, his successor David's reaction preserves some honor for the felled king. David kills the Amalekite for slaying YHWH's anointed and proclaims about Saul and Saul's son Jonathan, "How the mighty have fallen!"

King Saul's death is foretold by the ghost of the dead prophet Samuel, called forth by an unnamed woman from En-dor in 1 Samuel 28. In chapter two, I write that King Saul and the prophet Samuel are intertwined characters from birth to death. The Bible, I argue, intentionally entwines the characters of Saul and Samuel, king and prophet, because Samuel's primary role is to bring the people's request for a king before God and then to anoint that king. Their fraught relationship reflects the Bible's fraught relationship with the monarchy—a problematic institution if viewed as a rejection of God's rule.[1]

In this chapter, I argue that the entanglement of these characters—Saul and Samuel, along with Hannah (Samuel's mother) and the medium from En-dor—is a literary device that portrays Israel's first king as an equivocal character who is a victim and a villain, honored and condemned. How one views Saul, I assert, is connected to how these characters who form a literary network, evident in 1 Samuel 28, engage with or respond to Saul. It is particularly hard to separate the fate of Saul from the actions and reactions of Samuel, and thus it is hard to discern what conforms to divine will and what defies it. No doubt Saul's defiance of Samuel can be viewed as a defiance of God. Alternatively, Saul's disobedience and rejection could be viewed as essential to David's selection and God's plan for Israel. An equivocal reading of 1 Samuel 28 illuminates the complexity of Saul's character and the complexity of what it means to serve God.

The Equivocal King

From the moment his story begins, Saul appears to be a fraught and equivocal figure—both from the narrative's internal perspective and from the perspective of its readers. Saul equivocates as a character. He seems to both love and hate being king. The Israelite people may have asked for a king, but Saul never asked to be one. He neither seeks nor seems to desire kingship. In fact, he hides from

---

1 This is in fact what God says to Samuel in 1 Sam 8:7.

the prospect of becoming king.[2] Yet once he is king, Saul fights tooth and nail, without the possibility of succeeding, to maintain his position.

Saul is also an equivocal figure from a reader's perspective. Throughout his life, Saul seems unable to make a good, let alone a right, decision. His motives and actions are difficult to assess, making it difficult for readers to condone or condemn them and difficult for them to decide how to view Saul's character. For example, in 1 Samuel 13, Saul offers sacrifices at Gilgal before the prophet Samuel arrives. Samuel views this as an act of disobedience. Technically, it is because Samuel commands Saul in 1 Samuel 10:8 to refrain from sacrificing until Samuel arrives. Yet offering sacrifices when Saul does so is also a smart military move. The Philistines were gathering in Gilgal for war against Israel, and Saul was losing his army as soldiers were running away to hide. He offers sacrifices presumably to rally his troops and God to prepare for battle. His intentions seem to be good even if he disobeys Samuel.

Similarly, Saul's refusal to kill the Amalekite King Agag in 1 Samuel 15 could be understood in various ways—as an act of treason, cowardice, or compassion. God clearly commands Saul to take vengeance and wipe out the Amalekites. Saul must spare no one and nothing—no man, woman, or child; no ox, camel, or donkey. Saul should not have spared Agag, as well as the choice animals, as he in fact does. In 1 Samuel 15:21, Saul explains to Samuel why he saves the animals, claiming that the *troops* saved them with the intent of sacrificing them to God. With this explanation, Saul deflects responsibility and expresses good intentions. Yet the explanation does not address why Saul saves Agag, which leaves this act open to interpretation. Perhaps this conflicted and beleaguered king felt some compassion for the captured king.

Depending on one's perspective as a reader, King Saul could be a tragic hero, a villain, or a stooge. It is notably easier to justify a given reader's perception of Saul than it is to determine what the Bible thinks of him. Though the Bible condemns many of his actions, it also appears to have compassion for the man who never wanted to be king. King David certainly expresses compassion,

2 1 Sam 10:22.

admiration, and appreciation for Saul when he laments Saul's death in 2 Samuel 1:23–24:

> Saul and Jonathan, beloved and cherished, in their lives and in their deaths, they never parted. Swifter than eagles and stronger than lions! Daughters of Israel, weep for Saul who dressed you in crimson and finery and who decked you with gold jewels upon your clothes.

Despite David's praise, Saul may be a more appealing figure to a contemporary audience drawn to lovable losers than he was to an ancient audience. An ancient audience may have less tolerance for his weakness and failure. However, Saul's ineptitude paves the way for David's grace and success and, therefore, should be considered a necessary feature, if not a positive good, in the Bible's narrative—not unlike how I understood the role of Potiphar's wife in the Joseph narrative. Potiphar's wife may have done something "wrong" by repeatedly propositioning Joseph and then accusing him of rape, but her actions propel the narrative forward and enable Joseph to fulfill his fate. Saul's actions also propel his narrative forward, enabling David to fulfill his fate.

THE EQUIVOCAL MEDIUM FROM EN-DOR

The presence of the female medium at the end of Saul's life baffles many readers. Like Saul, she is an equivocal figure. On the one hand, her engagement with the dead violates biblical law (Lev 19:31; 20:6, 27; Deut 18:9–10) and Saul's own decree in 1 Samuel 28:3. This suggests that her presence at the end of his life adds to Saul's disgrace. On the other hand, her efforts to conjure the dead are effective, and she behaves kindly toward Saul, which suggests that her caring presence may mitigate his disgrace.

Uriel Simon views the medium and the prophet Samuel as narrative counterparts that form a triangular relationship with Saul in 1 Samuel 28. Simon sees the compassionate woman, "the kind witch," in contrast to the damning or "stern" prophet Samuel, suggesting that together, the characters temper how readers respond to Saul. Simon asserts that the two characters "complement each other in the mind of the reader, who thanks to his identification with each one separately, attains a true amalgam of rejection and acceptance, justification of divine judgment and empathy."[3] By perceiving harsh judgment against and compassion toward Saul as intentionally coexisting in the narrative, Simon offers an equivocal reading of 1 Samuel 28, similar to the one I will discuss that enables the Bible and its readers simultaneously to condemn and have compassion for King Saul.

Similarly, Joseph Blenkinsopp recognizes how the efficacy and kindness of the "Mistress of the Spirits" work to soften the Bible's overall condemnation of Saul. Blenkinsopp notes how the narrative "was intended as a contribution to the negative historiographical tradition about Saul, yet it points beyond itself . . . to engage our sympathies and to remind us of the ambiguities of the theology underlying these narratives."[4] Like Simon and Blenkinsopp, I recognize the emotional complexity of 1 Samuel 28 and suggest that this narrative offers a sympathetic portrayal of a doomed and flawed man. In my reading, the female medium is not only the measure of mercy that engages readers' sympathies for Saul. She is not simply the compassionate counterpoint to Samuel's justice. Rather, the woman functions as a part of a network of characters that includes Saul, Samuel, and Hannah. Together, these characters tell a complex story about individuals who are not portrayed as purely good or bad, as wholly condemned or respected.

As a midwife of death, the female medium helps exact justice for a man rejected by God. In this way, she serves God. Yet her unorthodox methods prevent her from being fully aligned with God. Instead, she is more aligned with Saul and is emblematic of Saul's failures. Her alignment with Saul may be why the woman behaves compassionately toward him at the end of his life, just as Saul's alignment with Agag may have caused him to behave compassionately toward the Amalekite king. The woman's care for and feeding of Saul at the end of his life, which evoke Hannah's actions

---

3 Uriel Simon, "The Stern Prophet and the Kind Witch," *Prooftexts* 8, no. 2 (1988): 168.

4 Joseph Blenkinsopp, "Saul and the Mistress of the Spirits (1 Samuel 28:3–25)," in *Sense and Sensitivity: Essays on Reading the Bible in Memory of Robert Carroll*, ed. Alastair G. Hunter and Phillip R. Davies (New York: Sheffield Academic, 2002), 62.

in 1 Samuel 1, soften the Bible's condemnation of this failed king and suggest that King Saul along with Samuel, Hannah, and the medium from En-dor—despite their flaws and judgments—all serve God and play a valued role in Israel's story.

AN EQUIVOCAL READING OF 1 SAMUEL 28: DEAD MAN RISING

The story begins in 1 Samuel 28:3–4:

> Samuel had died and all Israel mourned for him. They buried him in his own town of Ramah. Now Saul had removed the *ovot* and *yidonim* from the land. The Philistines gathered, entered and camped at Shunem. Saul and all of Israel gathered and camped at Gilboa.

Samuel's death and burial are recorded in 1 Samuel 25:1. Thus the mention of Samuel's death at this point does not inform the reader but rather serves to frame the narrative that follows. Samuel's death has consequences. In response, Saul removes the tools of divination from the land. Although scholars work to identify precisely the *ovot* and *yidonim*, most agree that they relate to spirits of the dead.[5] Interpreters must consider why Samuel's death results in Saul's removal of the means to engage with these spirits.

---

5 Robert Miller writes, "Interpretation of the term, אוב, has been either as spirits of the dead, perhaps related to אב if they are fathers or ancestor spirits, or an instrument for communion with the dead, such as a ritual pit. The latter reflects Mesopotamian, especially Hurrian etymology, while the former would fit the description of necromancy in Deut 18 as שאל אוב. In this case, it is a synonym for Rephaim, and the witch is a Rephaim-Master. What the witch sees rising up is an אלהים, but this term is used for ancestors in Isa 8:19–20 and for the spirits of tombs in Job 12:6." See Robert Miller, "The Witch at the Navel of the World," *ZAW* 129, no. 1 (2017): 98. Frymer-Kensky considers an *'ôb* to be "a technology for communication with the dead." She writes, "The story doesn't tell us how the necromancer conjured Samuel. That is left as the secrets of the trade, and it is only through comparative studies that we conclude that the *'ôb* might be a pit or trench that the necromancer filled with blood or animal parts or possibly a skull filled with the same." Tikva Frymer-Kensky, *Reading the Women of the Bible: A New Interpretation of Their Stories* (New York: Schocken, 2002), 312.

Saul's motivation is not explicit in the narrative; therefore, his action invites an equivocal interpretation. On the one hand, the removal of the means to engage with the dead may be viewed as an act of self-preservation that borders on deception. Perhaps Saul does not want the people to know that Samuel removed the kingship permanently from him, and therefore, he prevents anyone from having contact with the dead prophet. Saul may want to convince the people that God has not rejected and abandoned him. On the other hand, Saul's removal of the tools of divination could be an act of piety, even at his own expense. Leviticus 19:31; 20:6, 27; and Deuteronomy 18:11 prohibit engaging with these spirits.[6] Saul's prohibition may be a futile effort to conform to biblical law and to redeem himself even if it means that he has no other way to obtain prophecy, as the story demonstrates. With his prophet dead, Saul has no legitimate way of communicating with God. His prohibition denies him the only effective, albeit illegitimate, way to engage directly with God.

Yet with the Philistines gathering at Shunem, Saul feels he must speak to God. He grows desperate in 1 Samuel 28:5–7:

> Saul saw the Philistine camp and was afraid. His heart trembled greatly. Saul inquired of YHWH [וישאל שאול], but YHWH did not respond to him—neither in dreams nor through the Urim or through prophets. Saul said to his servants: "Seek for me a female medium and I will go to her and inquire of her." His servants said to him: "Indeed there is a female medium at En-dor."

---

6 Scholars debate how prominent "cults of the dead" were in ancient Israel, often using these practices to distinguish between popular and official religion. The biblical prohibitions of necromancy are seen as products of official religion. Francesca Stavrakopoulou challenges this distinction: "Indeed, the persistent 'popularizing' of rituals associated with the dead is particularly curious given the near certainty that mortuary practices of some sort or another were performed at all levels of society by all social groups, however configured. After all, everybody dies. It might thus be expected that death cults would be treated as a more normative and mainstream aspect of religious practice, so that the only justification for their being termed 'popular' would be their widespread, common occurrence." Francesca Stavrakopoulou, "'Popular' Religion and 'Official' Religion: Practice, Perception, Portrayal," in *Religious Diversity in Ancient Israel and Judah*, ed. Francesca Stavrakopoulou and John Barton (New York: T&T Clark, 2010), 45.

Facing his enemy, Saul is afraid. Arguably, fear has defined Saul's life and could be considered his most serious and fatal flaw rather than disobedience. He hides in fear when initially called to service in 1 Samuel 10:22. In 1 Samuel 15:24, Saul admits that he disobeyed God because he feared his own people and obeyed them instead of God. This fear may have lost Saul the kingship.

Now once again facing an existential crisis, the frightened Saul desperately wants to listen to God. He tries legitimate means without success and so turns to illegitimate means and asks for a female medium. Blenkinsopp notes that Saul's specific request for a *female* medium suggests that "such mediums and controls were more often than not female."[7] Blenkinsopp may be right that a female medium is a more likely option in the ancient world but that does not fully explain why Saul asks specifically for a woman medium. He could have asked for any medium—male or female—and been satisfied. Saul's desire to engage a female medium may be an effort to ensure that his actions remain under the radar in male-centric Israel. Despite a few brief mentions of female prophets in the Bible,[8] women religious professionals do not appear to be central to official Israelite religion. One assumes that a female medium would be more marginal and, therefore, less likely than a male medium to tell anyone that she consulted the dead for the king. Also, a woman might be more easily overpowered by a powerful male like the king, who could coerce her to risk her life to obey him. Notably, this does not happen. As we see, the female medium overpowers the king.

These explanations are tactical and speak to Saul's determination to obtain the information he requires with little cost to his reputation. Yet Saul also may want to engage with a female medium for her compassion rather than for her compliance. Abandoned by

---

7 Blenkinsopp, "Saul and the Mistress," 53. He continues, "The role of female prophet (נביאה) is attested (Exod. 15.20; Judg. 4.4; 2 Kgs 22.14; Neh. 6.14), and some forms of gender-specific prophecy were not clearly distinguished from divination (Ezek. 13.17–23). Sorcery (כשפים), including the ability to inflict physical and psychic harm, was also regarded as primarily a female domain (Exod. 22.14; 2 Kgs 9.22; Isa. 47.9, 12; Nah. 3.4), though we will bear in mind that the information comes to us filtered through immemorial prejudice." Ibid.

8 The Bible identifies prophets Miriam (Exod 15:20), Deborah (Jud 4:4), Huldah (2 Kgs 22:14; 2 Chr 34:22), Noadiah (Neh 6:14), and the female prophet in Isa 8:3.

God and his prophet, Saul may seek a woman's care. Perhaps he senses that he is at the end of his life and wants a maternal figure to guide him forward to his fate. Whether intended or not, that is what the medium does. She functions as a medium for Saul as much as for Samuel, shepherding Samuel's spirit into, and Saul's spirit out of, this world.

As I mentioned, the medium is part of a network of characters that includes Hannah. Hannah and the woman from En-dor have a particularly strong connection. They both exist at the margins of Saul's life. Their stories frame Saul's narrative. We see in chapter two how Hannah brings Saul and Samuel's story to life through the explanation of Samuel's name, which seems more appropriate for Saul and entwines the characters from birth. Now the medium brings their story to its conclusion and shepherds both into death. The pairing of these women and their narratives relates to the demise of Saul, which is captured linguistically in verse six and plays once again with Saul's name. Hannah's story is about answered prayers, as Hannah makes clear in 1 Samuel 1:27 when she brings the child she prayed for to the Temple: "For this child I prayed and God granted me my request which I asked from him [ויתן יהוה לי את שאלתי אשר שאלתי מעמו]." Samuel, and by literary extension Saul, is the embodiment of a request granted. Prophet and king are answered prayers.

At the end of Saul's life, God does not answer his prayers (וישאל שאול ביהוה ולא ענהו יהוה). God's silence brings Saul to the medium, effectively eradicating Saul's character. He is nothing—his name means nothing—if God no longer responds to him. Saul heads off to find the woman in 1 Samuel 28:8–10:

> Saul disguises himself and put on different clothes. He goes with two men. They come to the woman at night. He says: "Conjure me a spirit! Bring up for me the one who I tell you to!" The woman said to him: "You know what Saul has done—that he has cut off the *ovot* and *yidonim* from the land. Why do you entrap me to get me killed?" Saul swears to her by YHWH saying: "Upon the Living God, no punishment will happen to you on account of this."

Saul's disguise has both practical and symbolic meaning. He disguises himself and travels at night so as not to be recognized.

Blenkinsopp suggests that Saul must disguise himself to pass safely through enemy territory on his way to Shunem.[9] The removal of King Saul's clothes at this moment also symbolizes the removal of Saul's kingship, as it does in 1 Samuel 17:38–39 when Saul offers David his clothes before David battles Goliath and in 1 Samuel 18:4 when Saul's son Jonathan clothes David in his garments and weapons.

In these examples, clothing symbolizes identity and the status and position that adhere to them, as it did in the Joseph narrative. The removal of the clothing from Saul and Jonathan and the dressing of David in their clothing suggests the removal of Saul's identity as king and Jonathan's identity as his successor and the transference of both to David. Saul does not dress someone else in the passage I analyze here, but his disguise—the removal of his kingly clothes—symbolizes the removal of the kingship. It symbolizes his disgrace.

Saul takes two men with him to visit the medium. The precise number is intriguing. Saul may have taken two men with him to serve as witnesses. Numbers 35:30 and Deuteronomy 17:6 and 19:15 mandate that there must be two witnesses to a capital offense to exact punishment. Leviticus clearly states that consulting spirits is a capital offense. By bringing two witnesses, we see once again how practical and tactical Saul can be. Their presence may work to strong-arm the woman into doing what Saul asks her to do. If she refuses, the witnesses could testify that she works as a medium despite the prohibition. Or they could serve as a guarantee that the woman does not accuse Saul later of consulting spirits, since he could always use their testimony against her. The woman certainly expresses feeling entrapped by Saul and that her life is threatened. Another possible reading is that the two men function symbolically as witnesses against Saul. It is Saul who consults the spirits and receives a prophecy of his imminent death. In the context of the greater narrative, Saul's demise and death result from disobeying God. Had he obeyed and listened to God, God would have listened to him and Saul would still be king.

Both the removal of Saul's clothing and the presence of two witnesses act narratively to prepare Saul for what happens next and

---

9 Blenkinsopp, "Saul and the Mistress," 52.

to communicate this to the reader. Saul, no longer king, awaits a death sentence for his actions. Despite the irony of swearing to a God from which he is estranged, Saul makes clear to the woman that punishment will not befall her, perhaps communicating his awareness that he must suffer the consequences of this action. The woman complies in 1 Samuel 28:11–14:

> The woman said: "Who should I raise up for you?" He responded: "Raise up for me Samuel." The woman saw Samuel, shouted loudly, and said to Saul: "Why do you deceive me? You are Saul!" The king said to her: "Do not fear. What do you see?" The woman said to Saul: "I see a spirit rising from the earth." He said to her: "What does it look like?" She said: "An old man ascends wrapped in a cloak." Saul knew it was Samuel and bowed low to the ground.

As many commentators note, the illicit act works. The woman conjures up the spirit of Samuel. Her success proves her legitimacy and the legitimacy of her craft. At least for this moment, divination appears to overpower prophecy. Yet according to Blenkinsopp, the woman's startled response reveals her own surprise at her success at having visually conjured up the prophet.[10]

Blenkinsopp believes the woman is a fraud. A typical ancient séance relied on its own form of smoke and mirrors to convince individuals they were communing with the dead. As Blenkinsopp observes, "The most important skill required of the medium was that of throwing the voice,"[11] not unlike a ventriloquist.[12] In Blenkinsopp's

---

10 Blenkinsopp writes, "The woman was terrified because neither on that nor on previous occasions of the kind did she expect to see anything. The crucial factor in these séances was that only the medium was expected to have a visual experience; the client heard a voice, but saw nothing." Ibid., 55.

11 Ibid., 56.

12 Tony Conrad and Tony Oursler describe the methods of an ancient ventriloquist, "The ancient ventriloquists sometimes used a resonant cavity in the ground, or a vapor vent, to misdirect attention and confuse the location of the voice. There was never a 'dummy,' or ventriloquist's puppet. Most often, bent over and speaking in a muffled tone, the ventriloquist would easily convince the listener that a voice was coming from a 'spirit' trapped in the ventriloquist's belly." Tony Conrad and Tony Oursler, "Who Will Give Answer to the Call of My Voice? Sound in the Work of Tony Oursler," *Gray Room* 11 (Spring 2003): 48.

reading, the woman did not expect to hear any sound she did not make herself, nor did she expect to see anything. Thus her success at conjuring the spirit of Samuel indicates that either the king or the prophet overpowers the diviner to make this happen.

Although the woman confronts Saul and accuses him of deception, Saul does not appear in control of events. He tells the woman not to fear but then asks her what she sees. Clearly, only the woman can see the spirit of Samuel and not Saul. This suggests that the woman is in control of the spirit and the moment. Her description identifies Samuel to Saul who bows to the ground in deference to the prophet. Now Samuel appears to have the most power and status in this scene. The medium defers to the king and the king defers to the prophet. The hierarchy is clear.

DEAD MAN WALKING

The woman may be able to see the prophet, but it is notable that the prophet bypasses the woman and speaks directly to the king in 1 Samuel 28:15–19:

> Samuel said to Saul: "Why do you bother me by bringing me up?" Saul said: "I'm in great trouble. The Philistines are fighting against me and God has turned from me and no longer responds to me whether through prophets or dreams so I called out to you to inform me what to do." Samuel said: "Why are you asking me? God turned from you and is your adversary. YHWH has done to you as he said through my authority. YHWH has torn the kingship from your hand and given it to your companion David since you did not obey YHWH and did not execute his anger against Amalek. For this, YHWH has done to you today and will deliver Israel your people into the hand of the Philistines. Tomorrow you and your sons will be with me. Also, YHWH will deliver the camp of Israel in the hand of the Philistines."

The prophet's harsh judgment is on full display in this exchange. Samuel's anger at being disturbed is evident as is his frustration with Saul for asking him to respond to questions that God refuses to answer.

Saul still does not seem to understand fully his situation. He asks Samuel to tell him what to do (מה אעשה) when God has already told Saul through Samuel what God has done (ויעש יהוה לו).[13] Angry and frustrated, the prophet offers a final word of doom. In one day, Saul will join Samuel among the dead. That is Samuel's last word. Implicit in Samuel's final prophecy is the true meaning of Saul's name—or at least the meaning of his name at this moment. The one who is the answer to Israel's request for a king (שאלים] 1 Sam 8:10), the one who asks for God's help before battling the Philistines (וישאל] 1 Sam 28:6), becomes the one who dwells among the dead in Sheol (שאול).[14] Strikingly, Hannah praises God as the one who brings people down into and raises them up from Sheol in 1 Samuel 2:6. Her praise is prescient of Saul's and Samuel's fates, providing yet another link in their lives and narratives.

Samuel may be justified in his anger at Saul. As God's representative, he speaks for God and administers God's will and God's judgment on this rejected king. Yet it is also possible to view Samuel as being overly harsh at this moment, reflecting his own accumulated feelings of frustration with Saul more than God's. Samuel experienced the people's request for a king as a personal rejection (1 Sam 8:6–7). Arguably, an insulted Samuel sets up the new king for failure in 1 Samuel 13 by delaying his arrival to Gilgal so that Saul must offer the prebattle sacrifice himself.

Being called up from the underworld may be the last straw for Samuel, who vents his personal exasperation: Why are you asking *me* (למה תשאלני)?! God already told Saul his fate *through Samuel* (כאשר דבר בידי). As Simon suggests, in this reading, Samuel is more upset with Saul for disturbing him and for not listening to him in the past than he is with Saul's necromancy. According to Simon, the prophet "expresses his bitter disappointment with the king who lacks the intelligence to comprehend and accept the

---

13 Multiple manuscripts read לך in place of לו. Simon observes, "The repeated use of the verb *'asa*, 'to do,' shows that this is the indirect answer to Saul's question: . . . 'What shall I do?' There is no way to avert the disaster since it is the Lord's way of requiting him for not heeding His voice and not carrying out His command." Simon, "Stern Prophet," 163.

14 In the Bible, Sheol refers to the underworld where the dead dwell. See Pss 18:6; 30:4; 49:16; 55:16.

message implicit in God's fatal silence," and "explicitly deplores Saul's absurd desire to force God to answer him."[15]

Despite Samuel's obvious frustration with Saul, he is stuck with him in death as he is in life. Although Samuel asserts that he has nothing to say, he offers Saul a brutal prophecy. Saul and his sons will join Samuel and dwell among the spirits the next day. But where does this prophecy come from, and why does Samuel give it? Samuel certainly presents it as prophecy by evoking God's name, and yet we do not witness God speak directly to Samuel. Also, it would be quite unusual in the context of the Bible for God to speak directly to the dead. As Psalm 115:17 suggests, the dead appear to be cut off from God.[16] If Samuel is not relaying a prophecy, then his words function more as a personal curse that condemns Saul to join Samuel in Sheol. If Samuel personally curses Saul, he does not administer divine justice and judgment. Rather, Samuel's death sentence of Saul becomes a cruel act stemming from personal resentment. In this reading, Saul becomes Samuel's victim. As such, King Saul elicits compassion—perhaps from readers, but certainly, as we see, from the medium who enables and witnesses Samuel's cruelty.

Saul responds physically to Samuel's words, which causes the woman to respond to Saul in 1 Samuel 28:20–22:

> Saul quickly fell full-body onto the ground. He was very afraid of Samuel's words. He also had no strength because he had not eaten all day and all night. The woman comes to Saul and sees that he is very frightened. She says to him: "Your maidservant listened to your voice. I put my life into your hand and listened to the words that you said to me. Now,

---

15 Simon, "Stern Prophet," 165.

16 The dead do not seem to have a relationship with God. See also Eccl 9:5. Jennie R. Ebeling describes the world the dead inhabit, "The dead were believed by the ancient Israelites to live in a dark and gloomy underworld called *Sheol.* . . . The deceased who inhabited *Sheol* forgot about Yahweh and could not praise him (Ps. 6.5); in addition, and perhaps even worse, Yahweh did not remember the dead who lived there (Ps. 88.4–5). *Sheol* was a physical place that had a road leading to it, possessed a gate and was like a prison. Needless to say, the living feared this place." Jennie R. Ebeling, *Women's Lives in Biblical Times* (New York: T&T Clark, 2010), 143.

listen to the voice of your maidservant. I will put bread before you. Eat so that you will have strength to go on your way."

Simon and Tikva Frymer-Kensky perceive the woman's actions at this moment to be kind and compassionate. Frymer-Kensky writes, "The necromancer becomes the very model of Israelite hospitality."[17] Simon similarly writes, "Her sin as a witch is one thing; her decency as a sensitive, generous woman quite another."[18]

The woman sees and responds compassionately to Saul's visible distress. The king, known for his great height, collapses full-body on the ground in fear and physical exhaustion—his posture reflects his demise. Saul has not eaten in twenty-four hours. The reasons for his fast are not given. He could be fasting to appeal to God before battle[19] or in repentance.[20] Either way, Saul fasts futilely. His efforts suggest once again that he simply does not understand the finality of his situation. God will not help or forgive Saul. Samuel certainly understands that reality. And the woman understands as well, as her actions demonstrate. She treats Saul like a dead man walking. Although she clearly cares for Saul, by her actions the woman may be serving her own best interests. She must raise Saul and get him out of her house so as not to be accused of illicit activity. As someone who engages with spirits of the dead, she also could be fulfilling a professional ritualistic duty.

Food was often used to gain the favor of the dead and to lure the spirits of the dead into the land of the living, as Jennie R. Ebeling describes, "in order to appease the dead so that they might help the living, the family continued to provide the deceased with food and drink. Sacrifices were offered to the ancestors at the tomb and in various other places, including at burial markers (Gen. 28.17–18), on hilltops (Gen. 31.53–54) and at shrines (1 Sam. 1.21; 20.6)."[21] Seen in this way, the woman is doing what she is

17 Frymer-Kensky, *Reading the Women*, 314.
18 Simon, "Stern Prophet," 167.
19 Judg 20:26.
20 1 Sam 7:6.
21 Ebeling, *Women's Lives*, 143. Deut 26:14; Pss 16:3–4; and 106:28 provide biblical support for the ritual of feeding the dead. Blenkinsopp challenges viewing the woman's feeding Saul as ritualistic; he writes, "In the modern commentary tradition rather too much has been made of this meal. By accepting the woman's

used to—engaging with dead spirits by feeding them. Her actions indicate that she views Saul already as a dead man and is caring for his spirit. Still, her care may be viewed as an act of kindness. Saul is to die with his sons. This woman may be the only living person who will tend to his spirit once he is dead by providing it with food and drink. Her efforts reflect kindness and respect for the rejected king. In this way she is like David, who mourns for his rival Saul and kills the Amalekite who dared to lift his hand "to slaughter God's anointed."[22]

Notably, the woman takes charge of the situation, inverting the hierarchy that was established earlier. She commands Saul to listen to her. She asserts that he owes her this obedience because she listened to him at the risk of her own life. The woman's insistence speaks to her commitment to caring for Saul. Yet it also indicates Saul's demise. The man who wants desperately to hear God's voice must listen to the voice of this female medium.[23] David indeed is right. How the mighty have fallen. Initially, Saul listens but does not heed her voice. His servants and the woman together must urge him to eat, and he complies in 1 Samuel 28:23–25:

> He refuses and says: "I will not eat." His servants and the woman urge him. He listens to their voices, gets up and sits on the bed. The woman has a well-fed calf in the house. She quickly slaughtered it. She took flour and kneaded it and baked unleavened bread. She served Saul and his servants. They ate, got up and went into that night.

---

offer Saul was not entering into a covenant with her against Yahweh, it was not a Passover meal, or a mantic sacrifice to the spirits of the dead, and it is a bit fanciful to represent Saul as becoming a child again and being fed by 'mother.' . . . If it had a ritual character at all, it would have been the kind of ritual that surrounds the last meal before execution of a person on Death Row." Blenkinsopp, "Saul and the Mistress," 57–58.

22 2 Sam 1:14. Despite their rivalry and the threat that Saul poses to David, David shows similar respect to the king in 1 Sam 24 and 26.

23 Esther Hamori notes, "The issue of who listens to whose voice—not just in the everyday sense, but in the sense of both hearing and heeding an authoritative voice—is a central theme throughout the text." Esther J. Hamori, "The Prophet and the Necromancer: Women's Divination for Kings," *JBL* 132, no. 4 (2013): 834–35.

At last, the king obeys the woman. The small detail that Saul gets up from the ground and sits on her bed to wait for the woman to prepare the food indicates his submission to her authority.

The details of the food she offers and its preparation suggest a ritual component to the meal. The woman from En-dor kneads flour and prepares unleavened bread and slaughters (ותזבחהו) a calf to feed Saul and his servants. The root זבח most often indicates a ritual sacrifice.[24] It suggests that this is more than a meal to restore Saul's strength. It appears ritualistic if not sacrificial, as if the woman is either ritually feeding the dead or offering a sacrifice. Perhaps the soon-to-be-dead king is symbolically on the altar waiting to die.[25] This final meal in Saul's life, which is offered by the woman, evokes the sacrifice Hannah brings in thanksgiving for having born Samuel and works to connect these characters. Hannah slaughters a bull and brings it along with flour (קמח) and wine to the temple in Shiloh in celebration of and gratitude for her child's birth. Frymer-Kensky remarks on the connection between the women that is marked by these ritual meals, observing how "the necromancer is the counterpart to both Hannah and Samuel, and her meal resonates with theirs."[26]

Frymer-Kensky's critical observation captures the complexities of these characters and provides insight into the particular role the medium from En-dor plays at the end of Saul's life. Hannah and Samuel shepherd Saul into the narrative and inaugurate Saul's life and narrative as king with a celebratory meal. It is fitting that Saul's story and life end with another meal, albeit a very different kind of meal in tone. This one is somber, not celebratory. Against his will, Samuel is present—if not for the meal itself, at least for the events that lead to the meal.

Hannah is a mother figure who brings Saul's story to life. The woman from En-dor is a mistress of dead spirits. She brings Saul's story to its conclusion and Saul to his death. Her presence and Samuel's and Saul's work collectively tell a complex story about complex characters. Saul is disobedient but sympathetic. He is shamed

---

24 See Gen 31:54; Lev 17:5; Deut 18:3; 33:19; 1 Kgs 3:3.

25 A bed (מטה) may have a similar symbolism in 2 Kgs 4:21 when the Shunammite puts her dead son on the bed of the prophet Elisha.

26 Frymer-Kensky, *Reading the Women*, 314.

by his demise and yet honored by the care shown to him by the woman from En-dor. The medium performs an illicit activity successfully. She wrangles Samuel back to life and shepherds Saul into death. Her actions may have brought a curse on Saul's life, but she then eases Saul into death. Samuel is the voice of judgment, but it remains unclear if he voices his own or God's judgment. Samuel's prophecy may be a last gift to a king who begs to know what will happen to him. It also could be an act of cruelty.

In any case, the rejected king is removed from the narrative, paving the way for his successor. Saul's final moments reflect his failures while also preserving a measure of dignity for Israel's first king. Saul may die a brutal death, but his life and service are honored by the woman from En-dor, who pronounces his doom and shepherds him to his fate with care and compassion.

CONCLUSIONS

It is possible to honor a shamed king. It is possible to serve God through one's shortcomings and even through one's acts of disobedience. Despite Saul's manifest failures, the Bible does not present him solely as an evil or despised figure. For better and for worse, Saul's character, fate, and story conform to God's plan for Israel and its kings. As such, the Bible has sympathy, and even respect, for Saul as Israel's first king, which is particularly evident at the beginning and end of his story as well as in the way other characters engage with Saul. Samuel and Hannah inaugurate Saul's life as an answer to a prayer. Samuel and the woman from En-dor escort Saul to a grim death. Yet whereas Samuel harshly inflicts death on Saul, the woman from En-dor eases his passage into the spirit world with solace and respect. Their stories and characters cohere to reveal the Bible's complex relationship to the monarchy and to Israel's first king.

I conclude this chapter from my vantage point as an equivocal reader who perceives and appreciates the Bible's complexity that is evident in Saul's story. As a feminist religious reader, I particularly value Hannah and the medium from En-dor as powerful figures who act as God's partners. I value the ways in which they model a form of divine service that validates their needs and desires and values their initiative. These women manipulate the passage into life and the passage from life into death to introduce and remove Israel's first king in accordance with divine will. I also appreciate the ways in which Saul and Samuel, like Hannah and the medium, model divine service. Their intertwined stories show myriad ways to serve God and contribute to Israel's destiny. Samuel serves God through his obedience but also through his judgment and condemnation of Israel's first king. Saul desperately wants to serve God and may do so best through his disobedience. His failures may be his greatest successes, enabling Israel's beloved King David to assume the throne.

As I wrote in my introduction, the Bible does not tell simple moral tales, nor does it present one-dimensional heroes or villains. Like Potiphar's wife and Joseph, Saul and the woman from En-dor are neither heroes nor villains. They are complex equivocal figures whose carefully constructed narratives manifest the complexities of Israel's national story and the complexities of what it means to serve God and help fulfill Israel's destiny.

Chapter Four

ESTHER AND MORDECAI

Despite its remarkable literary construction,[1] Esther may be the biblical book that is most ripe for an equivocal reading. An equivocal reading enables a text to embody different ideologies and to communicate complicated, if not contradictory, messages. Esther is an equivocal book. It is a book open to multiple interpretations with competing messages that reflect different ideologies.

Esther is a book that does not fit easily into the Bible's core themes or its overarching narrative framework. It is not concerned with establishing or maintaining God's relationship with individuals or with the community of Israel. As many readers note, God is not even a character in Esther. The book of Esther reads as a diaspora fantasy of Jewish triumph against foreign rulers, yet it is hard to discern if it purports a specific strategy for Israel's survival in exile. The book may support a strategy of assimilation and playing by the rules of a foreign regime to ensure survival. It also may support a strategy of revolt against that regime.

Sidnie Ann White observes the ambiguity of Esther's message and status in both Jewish and Christian interpretations and claims that "the reasons for all the ambiguity regarding the book

---

1 Linda Day describes the style and structure of Esther, "By means of thematic and semantic connections, the elements of the plot are carefully woven together into a seamless whole, and the work's skillful construction maintains the reader's suspense throughout. Frequent repetition of words, phrases, and entire sentences unifies the narrative. The book works as a whole, and, unlike many other biblical narratives, it is not easily or adequately divisible into discrete sections." Linda Day, *Esther* (Nashville: Abingdon, 2005), 4.

of Esther . . . are the result of misunderstandings concerning its purpose."[2] Just as we saw in the previous chapter that it is difficult to discern what the Bible thinks of King Saul, it is not easy (and may be impossible) to understand what the book of Esther intends. Unlike White, I do not think this is because we misunderstand these narratives. Rather, I argue, it is because they are intentionally complex and ambiguous.

Although considered to be a late addition to the biblical canon and an outlier of the Bible's central narrative, the book of Esther does have biblical analogues in the stories of Joseph and Moses. The characters of Esther, Joseph, and Moses all ascend to prominence within foreign courts. Yet whereas Joseph and Moses clearly enact divine will and play a critical role in the formation of Israel's identity as a nation, Esther seems to be a reluctant player in God's or Israel's story.

What distinguishes Esther most of all within this triad is her gender. Of the three, she is the only *female* to achieve prominence in a foreign court. Esther also is the only figure among the three with a narrative counterpart who arguably functions as the story's central protagonist and its true hero. Esther's cousin Mordecai rises to prominence in the foreign court along with Esther and becomes, like Joseph, second to the king. Mordecai's presence and purpose in the book contribute to its ambiguity by presenting an alternative hero to Esther and an alternative strategy for survival. Whereas Esther appears to conform to the laws of the foreign court and land, thereby hiding her Jewish identity, Mordecai refuses to submit to foreign authority and presents himself as openly Jewish at great personal risk.

Though the book bears Esther's name, Mordecai may be the book's central focus and "principal hero," as Jona Schellekens asserts.[3] In contrast to Schellekens, my equivocal reading of Esther allows for more than one hero, or to be more precise, for the *possibility* of more than one hero and more than one strategy for survival. Although my reading recognizes the ways in which

---

2 Sidnie Ann White, "Esther: A Feminine Model for Jewish Diaspora," in *Gender and Difference in Ancient Israel*, ed. Peggy L. Day (Minneapolis: Fortress, 1989), 161.

3 Jona Schellekens, "Accession Days and Holidays: The Origins of the Jewish Festival of Purim," *JBL* 128, no. 1 (2009): 116.

Esther is not the undeniable hero of her eponymous book, I make a case as a feminist reader for viewing Esther as the book's true hero. As I show, Esther's gender is essential to the narrative and to her status as a hero and may reflect the context in which the book was written. As White asserts, a female may be the best hero or "role model" for an exiled community. According to White, Esther's character traits and actions "that make her successful are those that a Jew must emulate if she or he is to be successful in the precarious world of the Diaspora."[4] I agree with White that Esther is the heroine of the tale, and I show that when it matters most, Esther overshadows Mordecai to become Israel's savior. My reading differs from White's in that I do not argue that Esther is the best hero for a subordinate population in the precarious world of the diaspora. Instead, I argue that Esther triumphs over Haman *and* over Mordecai. In my reading, Esther's strength does not reflect Israel's weakness in the diaspora. Instead, it is a triumph over, and therefore a critique of, the two social hierarchies that shape this narrative: the hierarchies of Jew and gentile and of male and female (whether Jew or gentile). Esther defeats Haman because she overpowers Mordecai, a Jewish male. Her story is as much about Jew defeating gentile as it is about female defeating male.

Gender Matters

Esther's gender is a significant factor in her story. In fact, the book of Esther may be the biblical book that most overtly employs gender as a narrative device. The book's initial episode with Queen Vashti is the catalyst for all that follows and puts gender front and center in the narrative. In the first chapter of Esther, Vashti refuses to obey King Ahasuerus's command to parade before his guests at a banquet. Incensed, Ahasuerus consults his advisors, who declare

---

4 White continues, "The Jews in the Diaspora also are in the position of the weak, as a subordinate population under the dominant Persian government. They must adjust to their lack of immediate political and economic power and learn to work within the system to gain what power they can. In the book of Esther, their role model for this adjustment is Esther. Not only is she a woman, a member of a perpetually subordinate population, but she is an orphan, a powerless member of Jewish society." White, "Feminine Model," 166–67.

that Vashti's behavior, an affront to all men, could incite wives to disobey their husbands. Klara Butting notes how the wise men reflect the ancient viewpoint "that the power a man exercises in the state corresponds to the power he exercises at home," which leads one "to believe that female resistance endangers the whole state."[5] The wise men conclude that the king must banish Vashti and find himself another queen. After this episode, Vashti does not appear again. Esther becomes her replacement. Narratively, Esther's relationship with Vashti is as equivocal as her relationship with Mordecai. Just as there are competing heroes, there are competing queens who may reflect different strategies in how they relate to authority. It is unclear whether readers should compare or contrast Esther with Vashti. It is possible to perceive Esther as completing Vashti's revolution or as succeeding in ways that Vashti does not. Vashti's refusal to appear before the king wearing the royal crown (כתר מלכות) foreshadows Esther's wearing of the royal crown (כתר מלכות), given to her by the king in Esther 2:17, and the robes of royalty (מלכות) Esther assumes when she risks her life and appears unannounced before the king in 5:1.

Remarking on the relationship between the two queens, Linda Day considers them "representative examples of strong women" living in a patriarchal system who "represent differing strategies for maneuvering within an unsupportive, even hostile environment."[6] Butting suggests that Vashti lays the groundwork for Esther, claiming that Vashti's story is "a living source" from which Esther "takes directives and plans for her own resistance."[7] Esther may learn from

---

5 Klara Butting, "Esther: A New Interpretation of the Joseph Story in the Fight against Anti-Semitism and Sexism," in *Ruth and Esther: A Feminist Companion to the Bible (Second Series)*, ed. Athalya Brenner (Sheffield, UK: Sheffield Academic, 1999), 241.

6 Day, *Esther*, 2. Day comments on Esth 2:17, "At the designation 'crown of royalty,' the reader cannot help but recall the previous instance of this same term, the item that Vashti refused to wear when modeling for the party-goers (1:11), and draw a comparison with Esther. The fact that Esther willingly accepts the role that Vashti rejected highlights the difference in personality between these two women. . . . The comparison expresses, perhaps, a hope on Ahasuerus's part that Esther will turn out to be a different type of queen than was her predecessor." Ibid., 55–56.

7 She writes, "Esther's plan would not be conceivable without Vashti's refusal. The prevailing sexist balance of power has been made public by Vashti's resistance and makes an analysis possible." Butting, "New Interpretation," 246.

Vashti's example of open resistance, as Butting suggests, or she may employ a completely different mode of engagement with foreign authority, as Day suggests.

Either way, it is important to understand how the opening chapter of the book sets the stage for what follows. Vashti's removal from the throne and narrative serves the primary purpose of providing a rationale for Esther's entrance. Vashti must exit to enable Esther to enter the narrative. It is important to recognize that readers have no idea why Vashti refuses the king's order and that Vashti's concerns (or her behavior, for that matter) do not transfer to Esther.

Unlike Vashti's, Esther's story is not about disobedience or revolution. She does not refuse the king or disobey him, as Vashti does. Esther's story is about obedience. Esther finds favor with the king, placates him, and makes him obedient to her will. Her story is about asserting power not rebelling against it. Notably, Esther's story does not actualize the wise men's concerns that Vashti's actions could incite women or bring scorn against their husbands. Yet the wise men's statement makes explicit the gender-related anxieties that frame the narrative that follows, making the book about the power dynamics of gender.

According to Butting, the opening chapter of Esther presents "totalitarian and sexist structures" but reveals how they are not the "natural order, but an order established again and again by force."[8] For Butting, Vashti's story illustrates how male dominance is not a given but must be asserted forcefully. Understanding this, it is ironic that the means of this assertion—the removal of Vashti—prove ineffective in securing domination. Instead, it makes room for Esther and her assertion of power.

This story has an interesting parallel with the story of Moses. At the start of the Moses narrative in the book of Exodus, Pharaoh, like Ahasuerus, expresses gender anxiety related to his dominance. Afraid the Israelites will become too numerous to control, Pharaoh issues a command that all male babies be killed while female babies can live. Ironically, women work to save the one male baby, Moses, who leads the Israelites to freedom. Midwives Shiphrah and Puah, Moses's mother and sister, and Pharaoh's own daughter ensure

---

8 Butting writes, "The protest of women can undermine the powerful system based on masculine arbitrariness." Ibid., 242.

Moses's survival despite Pharaoh's decree. Ahasuerus and Pharaoh go to great lengths to secure their power only to become more vulnerable. Their gender anxieties prove justified, though their means to address them are flawed. Pharaoh should have been worried about Israelite men, but he should not have underestimated Israelite women. Ahasuerus was right to be worried about assertive wives, but he should have handled his own differently.

Once the future savior is saved in Moses's story, gender is no longer a significant factor. In Esther's story, gender remains one. In significant ways, the focus and meaning of her story hinge on its gender dynamics, enabling its readers to draw different conclusions about who should be and who is the center of the narrative and what its message is.[9] My reading places Esther at the center of a narrative about how one woman asserts authority over all the men, averts disaster, and becomes Israel's savior and the book's hero.

COMPETING HEROES

Esther is one of only two books in the Hebrew Bible named for a female character. Ruth is the other. As I mentioned, there is debate whether Esther is the main character despite her giving the book its title.[10] Even feminist biblical scholars feel the need to justify identifying Esther as the central character. Linda Day asserts that Esther "is a focal point for the action"; "is the most engaging character, the one in whom readers most readily become interested"; and is the one "portrayed in the greatest depth."[11]

---

9 Michael V. Fox remarks on the rich history of interpretation of the book and its characters; he writes, "Beyond the numerous interpretations I simply disagree with, there are other readings that I consider fundamental misapprehensions—some of them quite disturbing—of the characters and their author. . . . Haman alone has evoked no contrary view and so gets no epigraph. These epigraphs and my rebuttal show that the qualities of all the figures in Esther are not a cut-and-dried issue. Like living persons, they can call forth conflicting opinions among different acquaintances." Michael V. Fox, *Character and Ideology in the Book of Esther*, 2nd ed. (Grand Rapids, MI: Eerdmans, 2001), 3.

10 A similar debate could be had about Ruth given Boaz's role in the book.

11 Day writes, "Esther alone is not static, but grows and develops in response to the challenges posed to her. She is the book's main character, and the one who is to

Like Day, White recognizes the complexity of Esther's character and considers her, not Mordecai, as "the true heroine of the tale."[12] In my reading, the question of whether Esther is the main character—the hero—is integral to the book and is not a question asked only by critics who are puzzled by the text.

The book of Esther *wants* its readers to consider both Esther and Mordecai as viable heroes of the story. My reading identifies Esther as the book's primary hero and argues that the book presents Mordecai as a viable contender so that Esther can be seen as triumphing over not only Haman but also Mordecai. Mordecai enters the narrative as its presumed hero in Esther 2:5–7:

> A Jewish man lived in the fortress of Shushan whose name was Mordecai, son of Jair son of Shimei son of Kish, a Benjaminite, who was exiled from Jerusalem among those that were exiled with King Jeconiah of Judah who was exiled by Nebuchadnezzar, King of Babylon. He cared for Hadassah—that is Esther—his uncle's daughter, for she had neither father nor mother. The young woman was beautiful. When her father and mother died, Mordecai took her as his daughter.

Mordecai is a character with lineage and history and therefore, one assumes, significance.

Although the chronology given would make Mordecai at least 114 years old, the text asserts that Mordecai was exiled with King Jeconiah.[13] Most indicative of his significance is that Mordecai appears to be a descendant of King Saul, although it doesn't make the connection explicit. Like Mordecai, Saul—whose father's name is Kish—is from the tribe of Benjamin. Again, the chronology does not work. More than two generations must separate Mordecai from

---

serve as an example for its readers." Linda Day, *Three Faces of a Queen: Characterization in the Books of Esther* (Sheffield, UK: Sheffield Academic, 1995), 10.

12 In opposition to viewing Mordecai as the central character, White writes, "Mordecai, while certainly a sympathetic character, is not successful because he refused to fit into the situation in which he finds himself. . . . We have found that androcentrism abounds in most of the commentaries on the book of Esther, with the author either ignoring the character of Esther or relegating her to a secondary position behind Mordecai." White, "Feminine Model," 166.

13 King Jeconiah was exiled in 597 BCE.

Saul. Despite this discrepancy, the book clearly connects Mordecai with Saul. This connection is made even stronger as the narrative unfolds, since Mordecai's rival is Haman the Agagite. In the previous chapter, I mentioned that Saul loses the kingship because he disobeys God's command in 1 Samuel 15 to slaughter every Amalekite man, woman, child, and animal, including King Agag. Saul, of course, does not kill Agag—the prophet Samuel does. As a result, Saul loses the kingdom for his descendants and loses his relationship with God. Pitting Mordecai, a descendant of Saul, against Haman, a descendant of Agag, adds a layer of Israelite history and lore to the Esther narrative. Saul and Haman are enacting a deep historical rivalry that was crucial to the national formation of Israel. This fact alone indicates that Mordecai is the intended hero of the story. He will right Saul's terrible wrong.

Yet an equivocal reading recognizes how Mordecai's textual relationship with Saul also detracts from Mordecai's status. After all, as I discussed in the previous chapter, Saul was a failed and rejected king. Associating Mordecai with this failed king does not obviously afford Mordecai honor, nor does it necessarily bestow honor on Saul. A repeat showdown between Saul and Agag through their descendants neither changes history nor seems necessary to restore Israel's glory in their exile.

Mordecai's adoption of his orphaned cousin Esther presents him as a compassionate father figure and provides more support for viewing Mordecai as the book's central character and true hero. The word אֹמֵן (2:7), which I translate as "cared for," designates non-biological guardians of children in the Bible.[14] Most notably, it is used by Moses in Numbers 11:12. Frustrated by the people, Moses angrily asks God, "Did I conceive this people? Did I give birth to them that you should say to me: 'Lift them to your bosom as a nurse [אֹמֵן] carries an infant' into the land that you swore to their ancestors?" Moses implies that it is God's responsibility to care for the people and be their אֹמֵן. The use of this word suggests that Mordecai is to Esther what God is to the Jewish people. Just as God adopts and cares for Israel, Mordecai does so for Esther. Ezekiel 16 further supports this analogy by describing God's adoption of the discarded baby Israel. Abandoned by her Amorite father and Hittite

---

14 2 Kgs 10:1–5; Isa 49:23.

mother, baby Israel lies naked in the wilderness until God passes by and adopts her in Ezekiel 16:1–6. This relationship develops over time and God marries Israel in Ezekiel 16:8, functioning as both parent and spouse. Notably, the Greek version of Esther, as well as rabbinic tradition, suggests that Mordecai marries Esther and therefore, like God in Ezekiel 16, functions as her parent and spouse.

Mordecai may be associated not only with Israel's God. His name also suggests an association with the Babylonian god Marduk. Interestingly, Esther's Persian name associates her with the Babylonian goddess Ishtar.[15] It is not unusual for an exile to be given a non-Hebrew name.[16] What is more intriguing is that both Esther and Mordecai have divine names derived from the Babylonian pantheon. Arguably, as the chief god of the pantheon, Marduk overshadows Ishtar, thereby suggesting that Mordecai overshadows Esther. Yet unlike Mordecai, Esther has a Hebrew name—Hadassah, which means myrtle.[17] Also, her Persian name plays with the Hebrew root סתר, meaning "to hide." As Timothy K. Beal observes, "In many ways the book of Esther is a book of hiding."[18] Throughout the book, characters hide their plans and identities from one another. Most importantly, God's presence is hidden in the narrative. Linda Day comments on the motif of hiddenness in the book, which manifests its theological ambiguity and "reflects the fact that God cannot often be seen clearly,

---

15 Fox comments, "Both Jewish principals have foreign names, Mordecai's derived from the Babylonian god Marduk; the name *marduka* is known from Achaemenid documents. The name Esther is derived from either the name of the Babylonian goddess Ishtar or the Persian word *stâra*, 'star.'" Fox, *Character and Ideology*, 30.

16 Fox writes, "This is not evidence that Mordecai and Esther were Babylonian deities or even that they were devotees of them. Jews in Babylonia sometimes received foreign names (e.g., Belteshazzar, Abednego [Dan 1:7]; Sheshbazzar [Ezr 1:8, 11]; Shenazzar [1 Chron 3:18]; and Zerubabbel [1 Chron 3:17]). Jews in Hellenistic times too were often given non-Hebrew names." Ibid.

17 In his commentary, Jon D. Levenson writes, "The name 'Hadassah' (missing in the Greek versions and in the rest of the Masoretic Esther) seems to mean 'myrtle' (cf. Isa. 41:19), and thus fits with a number of Hebrew female names derived from plant names (e.g., 'Tamar,' the date-palm)." Jon D. Levenson, *Esther* (Louisville: Westminster John Knox, 1997), 58. Day notes, "Even Esther's Hebrew name, Hadasseh, which means 'myrtle,' hints at her attractiveness—she is sweet as the scent of a myrtle blossom." Day, *Esther*, 48.

18 Timothy K. Beal, *The Book of Hiding: Gender, Ethnicity, Annihilation, and Esther* (New York: Routledge, 1997), 2.

and it is impossible from a human perspective to know whether God is present but hiding or is completely absent."[19] Arguably, the book's most famous line, which generations of readers understand as alluding to a hidden, not absent, God, is Mordecai's warning to Esther in 4:14: "If you keep silent at this time, relief and salvation will arise from another place [ממקום אחר] and you and your father's house will perish. Who knows if for this moment you assumed queenship?" Readers often read the word "place [מקום]" as referring to God even though, as Fox notes, rabbinic literature, not the Bible, refers to God as place.[20]

Although it is possible to argue that Mordecai plays the role of God by adopting and protecting Esther, I argue that the book associates Esther with God. This association supports Esther, not Mordecai, as the story's hero. Her connection with God makes Esther among the most unique female figures in the Bible. Esther acts for God, who is hidden in the narrative and, I argue, hidden in the character of Esther.

Hiddenness defines Esther not only in name but also, as Day observes, in relation to her identity, by her not revealing "her people or her kindred."[21] In Esther 2:10, Mordecai commands Esther not to reveal her Jewish identity while in the king's palace. In stark contrast to Esther, Mordecai identifies himself as a Jew to the king's servants when explaining to them why he refuses to bow down before Haman. Although it is unclear why being Jewish prevents Mordecai from bowing before Haman,[22] Mordecai's refusal puts his

---

19 Day writes, "The Book of Esther does not attempt to convert skepticism into faith but permits actions to remain in their theological ambiguity." Day, *Esther*, 18.

20 Fox, *Character and Ideology*, 63. White makes a similar observation although she sees this verse as referring to Divine Providence and not God; she writes, "God's control of events seems to be assumed in this verse, and the status of the Jews as God's chosen people is also assumed. However, the God of the book of Esther does not take center stage as a deus ex machina, as in the book of Daniel. Rather, this God appears to act through human beings, allowing them to take center stage and act as the instruments of their own salvation." White, "Feminine Model," 162.

21 Day writes, "The pun provided by her name sets up the expectation of concealment, and the reader will continue to wonder throughout the story why this character is hiding. Only in verse 10 does one understand what Esther is hiding, 'her people or kindred.'" Day, *Esther*, 49–50.

22 Levenson comments, "Since v. 4 can be interpreted to mean that Mordecai's Jewishness was the cause of his refusal to kneel and bow to Haman, and since idolatry seems an unlikely factor here, some scholars have seen the issue as one of ethnicity.

life and his people's lives in jeopardy. Esther's hiddenness in name and identity aligns her with God in the narrative while Mordecai's exposure as a Jew aligns him with the people of Israel. Given this, Esther has the role of hero-savior while Mordecai has the role of the one who is saved. In other words, *Esther* is to Mordecai what God is to Israel. Mordecai is the Jew who rises to prominence in the foreign court because Esther ensures that he does, just as God ensures that Joseph and Moses rise to prominence within their respective foreign courts.

Aligned with God, Esther is the book's hero. She is the force that controls characters and directs events for Israel's salvation.

DUELING SAVIORS

The dynamic between saved Mordecai and savior Esther is most evident in chapter 4. The chapter opens with Mordecai rending his garments in despair, dressing in sackcloth and ashes, and wailing. Typically associated with mourning practices, these behaviors communicate publicly his distress at the edict, issued by the king under Haman's direction, to massacre the Jews throughout the kingdom. Mordecai reacts as a Jew to the news. His distress communicates his identity. Throughout the kingdom, Jews react similarly. But not Esther. Esther exhibits distress only upon learning about Mordecai's behavior. Esther 4:4–5 relates her discomfort at Mordecai's public display:

> Esther's servants and eunuchs approached her and informed her. The queen was very distraught. She sent clothes to dress Mordecai and to remove his sackcloth, but he did not accept. Esther summoned Hathach from among the king's eunuchs who he appointed to serve her. She commanded him [ותצוהו] to approach Mordecai to learn what's going on.

The use of the word "command [צוה]" indicates an assertion of power. Notably, Mordecai commands Esther in Esther 2:20 to hide

---

Agag's nation, the Amalekites, had long been conceived as the archetypical enemy of Mordecai's nation, the Israelites or Jews." Levenson, *Esther*, 67.

her identity; now in 4:5, Esther attempts to command Mordecai through Hathach to hide his distress and not act or appear like a Jew. In other words, Esther now is commanding Mordecai to hide his identity.

Hathach finds Mordecai at the palace gate. Mordecai tells Hathach about the king's edict to kill the Jews and about the role Haman played. Mordecai gives Hathach a copy of the edict to show Esther. In Esther 4:8, Mordecai commands Esther (ולצוות) through Hathach to appeal to the king on behalf of *her* people (עמה). In other words, Mordecai does not submit to Esther's authority. Instead, he attempts to assert authority over her. At this moment, under the threat of genocide, Mordecai commands Esther to reveal her identity. Hathach relates Mordecai's message to Esther, who responds in Esther 4:10–12:

> Esther told Hathach to command [ותצוהו] Mordecai the following: "All the king's servants and every people in the king's provinces know that any man or woman who enters the king's presence in the interior court who has not been invited, there is one law—execution. Only the one that the king extends his golden scepter can live. I have not been invited to come before the king for the last thirty days." They told Mordecai Esther's words.

Esther refuses to submit to Mordecai's authority and, once again, attempts to assert authority over him.

In the context of the story, her refusal to risk her life and approach the king seems wrong and selfish and should displace her as the story's hero. Reluctant heroes are found elsewhere in the Bible, yet their reluctance is based on insecurities related to their effectiveness or worthiness as leaders and not fear for their personal safety.[23] At first glance and at this moment, Esther does not appear noble. It is important that Esther does not refuse to approach the king. Rather, she relates a chilling reality. If she approaches the king without being summoned, she most likely will be killed. This would not be good for her *or* for the Jewish people. Seen in this way, Esther may not be refusing to help her people. She may be telling

---

23 Moses and the prophets Jeremiah and Jonah are reluctant heroes.

Mordecai that his plan is insufficient to ensure her or her people's salvation. They need a better plan.

Mordecai responds in Esther 4:13–16:

> Mordecai speaks in response to Esther: "Do not think that you, among all the Jews, will escape with your life by being in the king's palace. If you keep silent at this time, relief and salvation will arise from another place, and you and your father's house will perish. Who knows if for this moment you assumed queenship?" Esther speaks in response to Mordecai: "Go [לֵךְ], gather [כְּנוֹס] all the Jews found in Shushan so that they can fast for me. Do not eat or drink for three days and nights. I and my maidservants will fast in this way. Then I will come before the king, though against the law. If I die, I die."

Clearly, Mordecai hears Esther's words as a selfish refusal. In his mind, she is unwilling to risk her life to save her people. In response, he appeals to her instinct of self-preservation by telling her that her life is in danger even if she does not approach the king. As I mentioned, Mordecai's words are among the most famous in the book and often are read as a statement of faith that God will save the people if Esther does not.

Yet if Mordecai expresses faith that God will act if Esther does not, he is drawing a contrast between Esther and God. Either Esther saves the people, or God saves the people. This contrast strikes me as unlikely given the overall message of the book, which is that humans are significant participants in determining their fate. Also, given the fact that Esther does approach the king to save the Jewish people, her actions cannot be viewed as being in opposition to God's actions. When viewed as an either-or, Esther's actions would mean that God plays no role in saving the Jewish people. In fact, Mordecai's words could be read as showing a lack of faith. He expresses genuine doubt that divine providence brought Esther to the throne. Who knows (מִי יוֹדֵעַ), Mordecai asks, if Esther's assumption of the throne was to save the Jews? The evil king of Nineveh expressed similar doubt (מִי יוֹדֵעַ) when he urged his people to adopt behaviors associated with repentance to avoid destruction in Jonah 3:9. Likewise, the preacher of Ecclesiastes expresses uncertainty that life has meaning (מִי יוֹדֵעַ).[24] King David expresses similar uncertainty when he fasts and weeps over his sick baby in 2 Samuel 12:22. Who knows (מִי יוֹדֵעַ) if God will have compassion and save his son's life? In this context, Mordecai's "who knows" seems more like a genuine shrug of uncertainty than an assertion of true faith.

In contrast to Mordecai, Esther does not equivocate. She states the chilling truth that her life will be endangered if she appears before the king uninvited. Mordecai reads this as a refusal. I read it as strategic. She informs Mordecai why his plan is inadequate. She cannot just appear before the king without certain preparations. Esther *commands* Mordecai to gather the Jews and to fast on her behalf for three days and nights.[25] She also will fast along with her maidservants. Not only does she assert authority over Mordecai at this moment by commanding him (Go! Gather!), but she also employs a strategy that demonstrates her efforts to control the situation. Like King David, who fasts while his son is sick as an appeal to God, so too does Esther fast and command all Jews to fast. Esther's fast should be viewed as a ritual appeal to God, like Hannah's appeal to God in 1 Samuel 1. Whereas King David expresses uncertainty that the ritual will be efficacious (who knows?), Queen Esther does not. Esther appears to have faith the ritual will work. Her willingness to risk her life at this point (אֲבַדְתִּי אָבַדְתִּי) indicates her faith.

Esther is unwilling to act without appealing to God—as Mordecai asked her to—because she knows she will die. Esther is willing to act after she appeals to God because she assumes she may or will survive. Mordecai expresses doubt. Esther expresses faith. Mordecai responds to her and does what she commands him to (וַיַּעַשׂ כְּכֹל אֲשֶׁר צִוְּתָה עָלָיו אֶסְתֵּר). In this moment, Esther asserts authority over Mordecai and he complies. After three days of fasting, Esther dresses in royal robes, approaches the king, and is received by him. From this moment on, the story is about the salvation and not the destruction of the Jews. After hosting banquets to which the king

---

24 Eccl 3:21; 6:12.

25 Fox comments, "Esther accepts the charge laid upon her. But she has not merely been cowed into obedience by Mordecai's authority or threats. She immediately issues commands—to Mordecai, in the second person, singular, then to the community, through Mordecai, in the second plural. She now behaves as Mordecai's equal and as a leader of the community." Fox, *Character and Ideology*, 63.

and Haman are invited, Esther successfully appeals to the king in Esther 7:3. She informs him that she and her people (אני ועמי) were destined to perish because of Haman. She reveals her identity and stands with her people before the king. Haman's plot unravels, and he is hung on the gallows intended for Mordecai.

The tables have turned for Haman and Mordecai, but unfortunately, a king's decree is not overturned easily. Instead of annulling the first decree, the king must issue a new decree that allows the Jews to fight for their lives. The conclusion of the book is a bloodbath in which the Jews fight throughout the king's provinces, killing tens of thousands. Although they wreak havoc, the Jews do not entirely defeat their enemies and assume leadership. Rather, they prevent their national destruction and secure a position within the kingdom. Esther and Mordecai's high positions in the court will ensure the continued welfare of their people.

AN EQUIVOCAL ENDING

If the story ended with Esther's appeal to the king and takedown of Haman, she would be the story's uncontested hero and Israel's savior. Yet the book's conclusion does not identify Esther undeniably as its hero. It does not present her as exclusively triumphant. Instead, it presents an equivocal ending by suggesting that Esther's power and authority are compromised, as Esther 8:1–2 illustrates:

> That day King Ahasuerus gave to Queen Esther the house of Haman, the enemy of the Jews. Mordecai came before the king, for Esther told him what he was to her. The king removed his ring which he had taken back from Haman and gave it to Mordecai. Esther put Mordecai in charge of Haman's property.

King Ahasuerus divides the spoils and gives Queen Esther Haman's property and Mordecai his signet ring. It is unclear which is more valuable, land or political status, and who is more powerful, the queen or the prime minister.

Butting offers an equivocal conclusion. Esther may have more power, but Mordecai wields his power publicly; she writes, "Esther has gained her own wealth and the power of a house of her own. Her fight against Haman, the hater of the Jews, has undermined the power of those who want to see a man rule over his home and assert his authority (1:22). Outwardly, the sexist pattern remains the same. Esther appoints Mordecai to be in charge of Haman's estate and the king appoints him prime minister."[26] Alice Bach similarly concludes that Esther "must siphon power from Ahasuerus and gradually replace herself with Mordecai . . . as a male Jew maintaining power within a foreign nation."[27] Both Bach and Butting assert that Esther cedes power to Mordecai in the end. White agrees and suggests that this reflects the dynamic of Jewish life in the diaspora.[28]

I suggest that while Esther yields power to Mordecai, she does not submit to his authority. The book's conclusion presents an image of shared authority in which Esther maintains the upper hand over Mordecai. There is no doubt that Mordecai's status in the kingdom after the bloodshed is elevated. With Haman defeated, the playing field between Mordecai and Esther is *more* level in the public's eye. But the dynamic between Mordecai and Esther established in chapter 4 remains.

Esther continues to command Mordecai. She puts him in charge of her property. He essentially works for her. Even King Ahasuerus recognizes this in Esther 8:7–8:

> King Ahasuerus said to Queen Esther and to Mordecai the Jew: "Indeed I gave Haman's property to Esther and they hung him for attacking the Jews. Now you both write to the Jews what you think is right in the name of the king and you both seal it with the king's ring, for that which is written in the name of the king and sealed with the king's ring cannot be revoked."

---

26 Butting, "New Interpretation," 247.

27 Alice Bach, *Women, Seduction, and Betrayal in Biblical Narrative* (New York: Cambridge University Press, 1997), 192.

28 White writes, "Esther now disappears from our original story, leaving the final business to Mordecai. Her conduct throughout the story has been a masterpiece of feminine skill. From beginning to end, she does not make a misstep. . . . She is a model for successful conduct of life in the often uncertain world of the Diaspora." White, "Feminine Model," 173.

King Ahasuerus states that Esther, and Esther alone, owns Haman's property. It is notable that he charges *both* Mordecai and Esther to write the decree and to seal it with the King's ring, even though Mordecai is the owner of the ring. The king commands them to share political power. Despite this, Mordecai takes charge and alone dictates the edict to the king's scribes and seals it with the king's ring. This appears to be a blatant power grab in which Mordecai attempts to eclipse Esther. He even dresses in royal robes in Esther 8:15 as Esther did in 5:2, presenting himself as prime minister and monarch. Mordecai's power and reputation grow throughout the land, as Esther 9:4 relates, "Indeed, Mordecai was great in the king's house. His reputation grew among all the provinces, for the man Mordecai was growing greater." Day comments on Mordecai's enhanced profile, suggesting that his "greatness" refers to his growing reputation and not to the growth of "raw political power."[29]

In response to the edict, on the thirteenth of Adar, the Jews kill hundreds in the city of Shushan. At the end of the day of destruction, the king addresses Esther and, in my reading, redirects authority to her in Esther 9:12–14:

> The King said to Queen Esther: "In the city of Shushan, the Jews killed 500 men and the ten sons of Haman. What must have been done in the rest of the kingdom? What now do you request? It will be given to you. What more do you seek? It will be done." Esther said: "If it please the king, may tomorrow be given to the Jews to do what was done today and may the ten sons of Haman hang upon the tree." The king ordered this to be done, and the law was declared in Shushan. The ten sons of Haman were hung.

This passage indicates that Mordecai's initial decree was insufficient to ensure Jewish salvation. Esther must ask the king to issue another decree to allow the Jews to slaughter more inhabitants of Shushan.

The king grants Esther her request (מה שאלתך). Several times before, the king has asked Esther what she desires and then

---

29 Day, *Esther*, 148. Fox comments, "The officials fear Mordecai because he is powerful and famous and growing increasingly so. This sentence seems to be based on Exod 11:3, 'the man Moses was very great.'" Fox, *Character and Ideology*, 109.

granted her requests.[30] The language of request is evocative of the Saul narrative, in which God grants the people their request for a king only to reject him in time. As 1 Samuel 28:6 relates, God no longer responds to the rejected king (וישאל שאול ביהוה ולא ענהו יהוה). In contrast, Ahasuerus responds to Esther's request for another day of slaughter. Not only does this make Esther the ultimate savior of the Jewish people, but it also links Esther to the historic drama of the Saul narrative, suggesting that it is Esther and not Mordecai who defeats Agag's descendants and overturns Saul's fate. Esther dooms Haman. Esther inherits his property. Esther destroys his sons. Esther is the one whose requests are answered.

Once again, if the narrative ended here, Esther would appear to be its hero and savior. Yet after the destruction, there is celebration in Shushan. Mordecai records the events and then sends dispatches throughout the kingdom declaring the fourteenth and fifteenth of Adar national holidays of celebration and feasting. Many readers consider the book at large to be an etiology for the Jewish holiday of Purim, as opposed to a historical account of a battle won and a people saved. As I mentioned, Schellekens suggests the holiday originally celebrated the accession day of Mordecai. At this point, attention certainly is brought back to Mordecai, who ritually defines the day in Esther 9:22–23:

> As on the days that the Jews experienced relief from their enemies, and in the same month in which sorrow became joy and mourning became celebration, they must observe them as days of feasting and joy, sending gifts to one another and presents to the poor. The Jews accepted the practice that they had begun, and which Mordecai prescribed for them.

Mordecai institutes a national holiday for generations of Jews, and the Jews obligate themselves to observe it forever.

Yet again Mordecai redirects attention to himself and attempts to assume authority. And once again, Esther intervenes and, in my reading, reclaims her authority in Esther 9:29–32:

---

30 Esth 5:3, 6; 7:2.

Esther, the queen, daughter of Abihail, and Mordecai the Jew, wrote to confirm the authority of the second letter regarding Purim. He sent letters to all of the Jews in the 127 provinces of Ahasuerus's kingdom, words of peace and truth to establish the days of Purim at their appropriate time, just as Mordecai the Jew and Esther the Queen obligated them to do, just as they confirm upon themselves and their descendants practices of fasting and lamentation. Esther's declaration established the practices of Purim, and it was written in a document.

This is a notoriously difficult passage, yet one thing is clear.[31] Esther has the final word. Her letter authorizes Mordecai's decree regarding the practices of Purim. She is the queen. Mordecai is the Jew. Esther has authority over Mordecai. Still, the book concludes with Mordecai. A brief epilogue mentions the Annals of the Kings of Media and Persia that record Mordecai's great acts and status in the foreign court. Mordecai is certainly the hero of the Annals. Esther appears to be written out of this history. Yet as Butting observes, she remains front and center and is the title character of the book of Esther.[32] Mordecai may get the final mention and the place in the Persian history books, but Esther gets the book's title in the Hebrew Bible and, as such, gets the final word.

Throughout the narrative, Esther consistently asserts her power and authority to save the Jewish people. She is aligned with God and, at a pivotal moment, demonstrates faith in God. For these reasons, Esther is Israel's savior and the hero of her story. She earns her place as the book's title character.

Conclusions

An equivocal reading presents a convincing interpretation of a text but allows for other possible readings that may draw different

---

31 Fox, *Character and Ideology*, 125–28.

32 She writes, "At the end of the book of Esther we are once again confronted with the social context of the story: royal politics and historiography's silence concerning power and women's history. The book of Esther takes its place in this patriarchal history and historiography—and participates in it. Still, this book bears the name of Esther and not of Mordecai." Butting, "New Interpretation," 248.

conclusions. I have presented an equivocal reading of the book of Esther that argues Esther is the book's hero while recognizing the ways in which Mordecai could be intended to hold this title. Certainly, the book presents him as a viable contender. For some feminist readers, my equivocal reading may have compromised Esther's unique position as the front-runner of her story. Recognizing two heroes indeed may diminish the status of each. Yet it also reveals a complex dynamic between Esther and Mordecai that raises interesting questions about how and why the story uses these figures.

The rivalry between Esther and Mordecai may be about survival strategies within the diaspora, as it is typically read, with Esther modeling greater assimilation within the ruling culture and Mordecai modeling the maintaining of a distinct identity. But their rivalry does more than present survival strategies for diaspora living. The rivalry between Esther and Mordecai broadens the focus of the book, making it as much a story about how a Jew can live in a gentile world as it is about how a woman can live in a man's world— or to be more precise, how a woman can overturn a man's world. Whereas Queen Vashti loses her battle against the patriarchy and her patriarch, Esther wins. Remarkably, Esther overpowers every man in her narrative—whether Jew or gentile.

Esther's victory over Haman and Ahasuerus may be the miracle that manifests God's providential care, yet it is expected. Of course the Jew bests the gentile in the Bible. Esther's triumph over Mordecai is the real surprise that distinguishes Esther from other biblical books. Esther acts for God to ensure Israel's salvation. An equivocal reading that recognizes the rivalry between Esther and Mordecai shows how Esther wins her place as title character and hero of her story. Esther's triumph is for Vashti as much as it is for all the women in Persia and Media. It is also a triumph, in the opinion of this equivocal reader who is eager and grateful to discover female saviors aligned with God, for all women throughout time.

CHAPTER FIVE

TAMAR AND JUDAH

Queen Vashti is considered a feminist hero by contemporary readers who applaud Vashti for her courage to stand up to King Ahasuerus. Vashti's refusal to obey the king's command is a rebellious act against a patriarch and a blow to patriarchy. Other biblical women like Vashti challenge patriarchs and patriarchy. Miriam challenges Moses's exclusive authority in Numbers 12. In Numbers 27, the daughters of Zelophehad challenge the laws that specify that sons and not daughters may inherit a father's property.

Perhaps the woman who stands out above all others—who knowingly risks her life to challenge the patriarch who controls it—is Tamar in Genesis 38. Tamar understands that her father-in-law Judah withheld his son Shelah from marrying her. In doing so, Judah prevents Shelah from fulfilling the laws of levirate marriage outlined in Deuteronomy 25:5–10, which prescribe that if a man dies without children, his widow marries his brother and their first son bears her dead husband's name.[1] In response to Judah's withholding of Shelah, Tamar secures her own position in Judah's house by disguising herself and tricking Judah into impregnating her. When Judah learns that Tamar is pregnant, he condemns her to

---

1 According to Eryl W. Davies, "name" was "closely connected with his property"; he writes, "The 'name' was clearly associated in some way with inheritance, and the purpose of the levirate marriage was therefore not simply to ensure the continuity of the family but also, by implication to prevent the alienation of the ancestral estate." Eryl W. Davies, "Inheritance Rights and the Hebrew Levirate Marriage: Part 1," *VT* 31, no. 2 (1981): 142.

die. She then surreptitiously informs Judah that he is the father of her child. Judah admits that Tamar was right to behave as she did and spares Tamar's life.

Like Vashti, Tamar is viewed as a feminist hero by contemporary readers.[2] Tamar's initiative and agency are overt and, unlike Vashti's, ultimately are rewarded. She has not one but two sons by Judah, one of whom is the progenitor of the Davidic line. It is harder for us *not* to see Tamar as the hero of her narrative. Yet an equivocal reader of the Bible who strives to integrate a generous and critical perspective must wonder whether the *Bible* perceives Tamar as a hero when she blatantly challenges patriarchal authority and does so by engaging in a sexual liaison prohibited by Leviticus 18:15–16. The end may justify the means in this case, but the means could be viewed as desperate measures and not as a laudable act.

Equivocal Heroes and Legacies

Arguably, Tamar's story and character function as a corrective to Judah's. If so, they reflect Judah's debasement, and the need to address it, more than Tamar's valiance. For generations, readers have noted the placement of Genesis 38 in the Joseph narrative and questioned the relationship between the two. In Genesis 37, Judah convinces his brothers not to kill Joseph but to sell him to a caravan heading to Egypt. Although Judah effectively saves Joseph's life, his question "What gain is there in killing our brother?"[3] suggests that Judah is more concerned with personal profit than with his brother's life.

Genesis 38 appears to interrupt the Joseph narrative by focusing on Judah, who departs from his brothers and starts a family. Yet as Robert Alter correctly observes, there are many literary connections between Genesis 38 and the rest of the Joseph narratives, most notably the use of the word "recognize," which appears in

---

2 Rachel E. Adelman writes about Gen 38, "Whatever the motives, the narrative is one of the most compelling accounts of female heroism in Genesis." Rachel E. Adelman, *The Female Ruse: Women's Deception and Divine Sanction in the Hebrew Bible* (Sheffield, UK: Sheffield Phoenix, 2015), 69.

3 Gen 37:26.

Genesis 37:32; 38:25; and 42:7.[4] These connections to the greater Joseph narrative suggest that Tamar's story is about Judah's redemption and that Tamar is a means through which Judah can be restored as a prominent patriarch ultimately worthy of being the ancestor of the royal line. Tamar's actions reflect the low point of Judah's life and are reprehensible, although her intentions are good. In this way, she resembles the woman from En-dor, discussed in chapter three, who nobly cares for King Saul but practices divination and, therefore, must be viewed as an outlaw.

Just as the medium's character and story are reflective of Saul's, so too are Tamar's character and story reflective of Judah's. Yet whereas the woman from En-dor provides comfort for Saul but cannot restore him to the throne, Tamar does succeed in redeeming Judah. As Mark Leuchter observes, "It is only through reconciliation with Tamar . . . that Judah is restored to righteousness and that the survival of his progeny is secured."[5] In this reading of Genesis 38, the children born at the end of the story become Judah's reward, not Tamar's. The retelling of the story in 1 Chronicles 2:3–4 supports this by numbering Perez and Zerah among Judah's five children. If Judah is considered the father of Tamar's children, then he does not perform levirate marriage. The sexual liaison with Tamar does not establish Judah's dead son's name or inheritance; it secures Judah's name and legacy. It also does not secure Tamar's position as a wife in the household.[6] Genesis 38:26 states explicitly that Judah

---

4 Alter writes, "This precise recurrence of the verb in identical forms at the ends of Genesis 37 and 38 respectively is manifestly the result not of some automatic mechanism of interpolating traditional materials but of careful splicing of sources by a brilliant literary artist." Robert Alter, *The Art of Biblical Narrative* (New York: Basic Books, 1981), 10.

5 Mark Leuchter, "Genesis 38 in Social and Historical Perspective," *JBL* 132, no. 2 (2013): 225.

6 Davies writes, "Thus the view that the levirate duty was limited to the one purpose of raising an heir for the dead is too narrowly defined to do justice to the nature of the obligation as presented in the Old Testament. That the primary object was to provide the widow with a male heir who would inherit the property of her deceased husband need not be denied, but it must be emphasized that this was not the only purpose behind the levirate duty, for by contemplating a marriage between the brother-in-law and the widow, the law would have ensured her protection and support even if she did not have [a] child as a result of the union." Davies, "Inheritance Rights," 144. George W. Coats posits that conception alone and not marriage is the right of widow, and that Tamar intended only to conceive by Judah and not

never again has sex with Tamar. First Chronicles 2:4 refers to Tamar as Judah's daughter-in-law and not as his wife. It seems that Tamar does not inhabit the role of wife in Judah's household.

Given that Tamar does not assume the role of wife, it is fair to say that Tamar functions only to have Judah's child and as such is "in perfect congruence with patriarchal interests," as Fuchs observes.[7] Fuchs perceives Tamar's story as fitting comfortably within the biblical trope of motherhood that I discuss more fully in chapter two, in which mothers proactively ensure the birth of a son and establish or reestablish patrilineal continuity. Fuchs observes how the "courage and wisdom of Tamar, Judah's daughter-in-law, results in the successful re-establishment of Judah's patrilineage."[8] Once sons are born, generally "mothers slip out of the literary scene and are rarely mentioned in subsequent narratives."[9] This is certainly true for Tamar, although with an interesting caveat. Tamar's story ends with the birth of her twins, but her name remarkably lives on through two subsequent characters. Several generations after Judah and Tamar, King David names his daughter Tamar. Second Samuel 13 tells the tragic story in which this Tamar is raped and then discarded by her half brother Amnon. Ruined, she remains the rest of her life "desolate in the house of her brother Absalom."[10] Absalom avenges his sister by killing Amnon, thereby tearing apart the house of David. Absalom also names his own daughter Tamar.[11]

Perhaps Tamar was a popular name in the ancient world, but its connection with three women significant to the Davidic line suggests a narrative intention. Tamar means date palm—a tree that, as Frymer-Kensky observes, "can bear copious and precious fruit." Frymer-Kensky further observes that "the fertility of the date palm is not assured" and that the date palm must "be pollinated by direct human action."[12] She concludes that the Tamar of Genesis 38

---

to marry him. See George W. Coats, "Widow's Rights: A Crux in the Structure of Genesis 38," *CBQ* 34 (1972): 461–66.

7 Fuchs, *Sexual Politics*, 73.

8 Ibid., 46.

9 Fuchs writes, "The birth of the son leads to the inevitable mimetic and diegetic death of the mother." Ibid.

10 2 Sam 13:20.

11 2 Sam 14:27.

12 Frymer-Kensky, *Reading the Women*, 266.

"has the *potential* to bear, but her fertility will be endangered" and that the "plot will determine whether she disappears (as did Tamar, the daughter of David) or becomes the ancestress of a precious hero."[13] Frymer-Kensky perceives a clear contrast between the Tamar of Genesis 38 and of 2 Samuel 13. Both strive for fertility. Yet whereas the Tamar of Genesis 38 achieves her aim and is "pollinated" by Judah, the Tamar of 2 Samuel 13 is not pollinated and is denied fertility.[14]

I view the Tamar narratives less as contrasting stories with the similar concern of fertility and more as a narrative continuum. I perceive 2 Samuel 13 to be a response to Genesis 38 and argue that the relationship between the central characters in these narratives, suggested by the repetition of the name Tamar, invites an equivocal reading. On the one hand, the latter Tamar could tarnish the reputation of the former. The Tamar of Genesis 38 initiates a sexual encounter that ensures the Davidic line. The Tamar of 2 Samuel 13 is violated sexually. This violation tears the house of David in two. It is possible to view the fate of the second Tamar as a consequence of, or even a punishment for, the actions of the first. Lest one think that a sexually aggressive female should be rewarded in the Bible, the fate of the latter Tamar presents a not-so-subtle warning of what will happen to such women. Ultimately, the sexually aggressive woman will be sexually violated. On the other hand, the repetition of the name Tamar can be viewed as a vindication of Tamar and the efforts she made to secure Judah's line. If Tamar attempts to uphold levirate marriage, thereby "establishing the name" of her dead husband as Deuteronomy 25:6 prescribes, it is ironic that the name that is established through generations of the royal line is hers.

Tamar's name lives on, providing her with a legacy. Although violated and desolate, childless Tamar of 2 Samuel 13 has a namesake through her niece. The repetition of the name Tamar may be the Bible's subtle way of rewarding the first Tamar. She, not her dead husband, receives the intended benefit of levirate marriage. I perceive Tamar in Genesis 38 to be an equivocal character in her

---

13 Ibid.

14 In contrast to Frymer-Kensky, Yoël L. Arbeitman links Tamar's name with the Hittite noun *dammara*, meaning "cultic functionary." See Yoël L. Arbeitman, "Tamar's Name or Is It? (Gen 38)," *ZAW* 112 (2000): 341–55.

immediate and in the greater biblical context. I offer a reading that recognizes the ways in which Tamar's story manifests her remarkable strength but also, like my reading of Hannah's story, acknowledges the ways in which Tamar's character is circumscribed by her gender.

My equivocal reading reveals a complex dynamic within the narrative, not unlike the dynamic evident in the book of Esther. Judah and Tamar engage in a power struggle akin to Mordecai and Esther's. Throughout their narrative, Tamar and Judah exert power over each other, as I will show, by attempting to exert power over the forces of life and death. They also serve their own distinct, and at times conflicting, interests. Judah works to preserve his existing family by protecting his living son. Tamar works to preserve Judah's patriline—his future family—as well as her place within Judah's household. Judah risks the future to preserve the present. Tamar risks her life and her present to preserve the future. Judah works to prevent death. Tamar works to ensure life. Tamar's interests align better with the Bible's primary interests in procreation and legacy.

In the end, Judah recognizes this. His recognition is a transformative moment in which he aligns himself appropriately with the Bible's central concerns and embraces life. Once he does, Judah assumes a position of power over Tamar and controls her life. Judah does not kill Tamar, nor does he sleep with her again. One imagines Tamar lives a rather isolated life within Judah's house or perhaps even in her father's house—a life not unlike the Tamar of 2 Samuel 13. Tamar of Genesis 38 may be justified in what she did. Her interests may be served, but her story concludes at this point with only echoes in her namesakes, while Judah's continues and is lauded for generations to come. She is an equivocal figure who helps steer Judah, another equivocal figure, back on course to sire the royal line that secures and ensures Israel's future.

An Equivocal Reading of Genesis 38: Judah's Descent

After having sold his brother Joseph to merchants heading to Egypt and having tricked his father, Jacob, into believing Joseph was killed by a wild animal, Judah heads off on his own in Genesis 38:1–5:

At that time, Judah went down from his brothers and camped alongside an Adullamite man named Hirah. Judah saw there the daughter of a Canaanite man whose name was Shua. He took her and entered her. She conceived and gave birth to a son. He named him Er. She conceived again and gave birth to a son. She named him Onan. Again, she gave birth to a son and named him Shelah. He was in Chezib when she birthed him.

Although Judah's life as a patriarch appears to unfold easily and appropriately with the birth of three sons, there are hints that all is not well. First, there is the description that Judah "went down" from his brothers (וירד יהודה מאת אחיו), which has a particular meaning in the greater context of the Joseph story. Joseph's story is about how he descends physically and in status before he ascends. His brothers cast him into a pit (בור) in Genesis 37:24 before selling him into slavery. Joseph then descends (הורד) into Egypt in Genesis 39:1, where he is accused of seducing Potiphar's wife. He then is imprisoned in a similar place (בור),[15] where he interprets correctly the dreams of Pharaoh's cupbearer and baker and begins his ascent in Pharaoh's court.

As I mentioned in chapter one, Joseph's descent and ascent mirror the nation of Israel's descent into and ascent from Egypt. In this context, Judah's descent cannot be viewed positively. Although he may be destined to ascend, as the parallels suggest, at this moment he is in decline. Also, the description makes clear that Judah separates from his brothers. Notably, the laws of levirate marriage in Deuteronomy 25:5 begin with "when brothers dwell together [כי ישבו אחים יחדו]." This phrasing could suggest that the brothers must be living near one another to require one to function as the levir for the other.[16] Judah's move away from his brothers indicates a willingness to disengage from his family and their concerns. It hints at a reality that becomes all too clear as the narrative progresses: Judah is willing to relinquish his family's name and legacy.

The place name also casts a shadow over Judah. Judah's third son is born in Chezib (כזיב). The root כזב means "to deceive."

---

15 Gen 41:14.

16 Gen 13:6 and 36:7 use similar language to describe physical proximity.

Deception permeates Judah's narrative if not his character. Yoël L. Arbeitman observes how the place name indicates "an actuality which directly leads to Tamar's need to repair to Judah himself for impregnation" and helps Judah move from deception to righteousness.[17]

The focus on Judah and the birth of his three children raises narrative expectations that are familiar to us from other patriarchal narratives. Obviously, infertility is not an issue in this story as it is in other patriarchal narratives. But succession could be. The central concern of the patriarchal narratives, and of the patriarch in question, is which son will receive the father's and God's blessings and ensure the continuity and thriving of the family's legacy. Sibling rivalry and deception are common features of the patriarchal narratives as the designated heir becomes apparent.

Initially, Judah appears concerned with securing his family's legacy when he marries his eldest son, Er, to Tamar. The story takes an unexpected turn in Genesis 38:6–10:

> Judah took a wife for Er, his first-born. Her name was Tamar. Er, Judah's first-born was evil in the eyes of YHWH and YHWH killed him. Judah said to Onan: "Have sex with your brother's wife, be her levir, and establish your brother's seed." Onan knew that the seed would not be his so when he had sex with his brother's wife, he wasted it upon the ground and did not give seed to his brother. What he did was evil in YHWH's eyes. He also died.

The text twice identifies Er as Judah's firstborn. Er should be Judah's primary heir. His marriage to Tamar should lead to securing Judah's legacy for another generation. Yet without specifying the reason, God kills Er before that next generation can be born.

As in earlier patriarchal narratives, with Er's death, fertility— though not infertility—is a concern. In response, Judah behaves like a good patriarch who takes matters into his own hands and commands Onan to fulfill the duties of the levir. Onan defies his father and spills his seed onto the ground. Onan's defiance compromises Judah's power and status. The patriarch's commands are

---

17 Arbeitman, "Tamar's Name," 342.

not obeyed, jeopardizing Judah's legacy. It is interesting that God, and not Judah, punishes Onan. Either Judah is unaware of Onan's wrongdoing or he does not care. He may prefer to protect his living son over his unborn grandson. At this point, Judah appears to be an ineffective patriarch who is not in control of his family and not working for the family's best interest by securing the next generation.

Also, the text subtly presents Judah in a negative light by suggesting his disregard for biblical law. Judah does work to fulfill the obligations of levirate marriage and, therefore, appears to demonstrate patriarchal instincts and concern. Yet the Deuteronomic text that outlines levirate marriage does not mention the father of the dead son. Levirate marriage concerns only the brothers, which may suggest that Israelite levirate marriage is enacted only when the father is no longer alive.[18] Admittedly, this is an argument from silence. But it is notable that the passage in Deuteronomy begins "When brothers dwell together" and makes no mention of the father. Also, the father does not seem to participate in the ritual that releases the brother from his obligation. The widow brings the brother before the elders.

As a point of comparison, there are two situations described prior in Deuteronomy in which individuals are also brought before the elders—the case of the rebellious child in Deuteronomy 21:18–21 and the case of the woman accused by her husband of not being a virgin upon marriage in 22:13–21. In both cases, the parents bring the person in question before the elders. The absence of the father in the Deuteronomic passage that prescribes levirate marriage suggests that Judah as a father may not have any obligation to ensure that it takes place.

Genesis 38 may even critique Judah for his initiative in commanding that it takes place. Judah orders Onan to have sex with his brother's wife (בא אל אשת אחיך). His words echo the prohibitions against sleeping with one's sister-in-law (אשת אחיך) found in Leviticus 18:16 and 20:21, suggesting textually that he is knowingly or unknowingly willing to violate them. Notably, the Deuteronomic

---

18 The practice is identified as *yibbum* from the Hebrew word יבם, which means "brother-in-law." Hittite and Middle Assyrian laws, which legislate levirate marriage, do allow a father-in-law to marry his son's widow.

passage on levirate marriage refers to the widow as "wife of the dead
[אשת המת]" and not as "your brother's wife"—an elocution that
deflects attention away from the Levitical laws and does not present
the custom as a clear violation of them.[19]

At this point, Judah may have good patriarchal intentions,
but his actions already seem haphazard, if not careless. He has no
qualms about separating from his own brothers and no hesitation
about encouraging a forbidden sexual relationship to fulfill a ritual
that may not be necessary while he is alive. With two sons dead,
Judah should be desperate to have Tamar marry his third son,
Shelah, to provide him with an heir. Yet his words to Tamar suggest
one thing while his actions suggest another in Genesis 38:11–12:

> Judah said to Tamar his daughter-in-law: "Dwell as a widow
> in your father's house until my son Shelah grows." For he
> said, lest this one also die like his brothers. Tamar went
> and dwelled in the house of her father. Many days passed and
> Shua's daughter, Judah's wife, died. Judah was comforted. He
> went up to Timnah to sheer his sheep with his friend Hirah
> the Adullamite.

Judah exercises power over Tamar by ordering her to return to her
father's house and dwell there as a widow. Judah also expresses emotional vulnerability, if not weakness. Having lost two sons already,
he fears losing a third and mistakenly blames Tamar. Frymer-Kensky
suggests that Judah "seems more foolish than evil" at this moment
and that his actions show how "a man with both power and lack of
understanding becomes an oppressor."[20]

To a contemporary reader, Judah's concern for his last remaining child is understandable. His behavior toward Tamar may even
be justified if Judah is viewed as a desperate father trying to keep his
son alive. But his actions look very different in the context of the
Bible, as Frymer-Kensky observes. He misreads the situation. Not
only does Judah blame the wrong person for his sons' deaths, but
he is unable to see their wrongdoing. Initially, Judah appears ignorant, and his ignorance jeopardizes his family's continuity. He does

19 A similar expression appears in Ruth 4:5.
20 Frymer-Kensky, *Reading the Women*, 267.

not know that Er is evil, and he assumes that Onan will fulfill his duty. God sees that Er is evil and kills Er. Onan spills his seed, and God punishes Onan for wasting his seed. Although still ignorant of God's role in the events, Judah banishes Tamar from his home and, this time, knowingly jeopardizes his family's legacy.

In the biblical context, it is difficult to overemphasize the importance of legacy and inheritance. Securing the future of a family and the nation of Israel is of paramount importance in the Bible. Children and land—progeny and property—were essential to the future of individual Israelite families and the nation. They are deeply intertwined concerns throughout the Bible, as Raymond Westbrook writes, "In ancient Israel, the principal source of income was not contract, as in modern society, but property, and the most important property for these purposes was agricultural land. At the same time, the principal economic unit was the family, which provided the framework for exploitation of the land and for distribution of the income from it."[21] Property and progeny are not only intertwined in biblical laws but also the substance of God's blessings to individual patriarchs and to the nation of Israel. God promises Abraham, Isaac, and Jacob numerous descendants and lands for them to inhabit forever.[22] Israel's future depends on protecting property through patrilineal descent. Given this, Judah's withholding of Shelah and his banishment of Tamar demonstrate a willingness to forgo the future of his family. His choice goes against biblical preferences and ideology and jeopardizes all of Israel. An ancient reader would know the significance of Judah's family and presumably would shudder at the risk Judah takes with his own future and the future of the Davidic dynasty. Judah may look powerful in this moment when he sends Tamar back to her father's house, but he does not look like an effective patriarch, let alone a righteous one. In contrast, Tamar looks less powerful, but her behavior redounds to her credit. Obedient to Judah, she dwells like a widow in her father's house. The use of the root "to dwell [ישׁב]" suggests an indefinite stay in her natal home. She has left her husband's house and is back in her father's care.

---

21 Raymond Westbrook, *Property and the Family in Biblical Law* (Sheffield, UK: Sheffield Academic, 1991), 11.

22 Gen 12:1–9; 13:15–17; 15; 17:1–8; 22:17–18; 26:24; 28:10–15; 35:10–12.

By sending Tamar back to her father, Judah appears to have relinquished any responsibility for her.[23] But Tamar dwells in her father's house specifically as a widow. Her ongoing status as a widow could be imposed on her by Judah, as Frymer-Kensky suggests, and as such disempowers her.[24] According to this reading, Judah dangles the possibility of marriage to Shelah without any intention of fulfilling it, thereby preventing Tamar from marrying someone else.

I offer another reading and suggest that Tamar's widow status could be self-imposed, which then empowers her character. Tamar may be unwilling to give up her identity as a widow to force Judah to act. Her widow's garb is a visible reminder of the promise Judah made and must fulfill. Also, the use of the verb "to dwell" evokes the Deuteronomic verse that introduces the levirate laws. Levirate marriage is initiated when brothers dwell together (כי ישבו אחים יחדו) and one dies without an heir. As I mentioned previously, Judah removes himself from his brothers' presence (וירד יהודה מאת אחיו) at the beginning of Genesis 38, suggesting that Judah does not value his family or, by extension, their patrilineage. In contrast, Tamar goes to dwell among her natal household, suggesting a loyalty and obligation to her family similar to the one manifested by a willing levir.

Tamar's Deception

Tamar's ongoing status as a widow dramatically contrasts her with Judah, who loses his wife and recovers quickly from his loss. Mention of the death of Judah's wife is immediately followed by mention of Judah's consolation, which is manifested by his sheep-shearing excursion. Sheep-shearing was a time for celebration in the ancient world. Judah's attendance indicates that he is not a sad or isolated

---

23 Marriage in ancient Israel was typically patrilocal. Married women joined their husbands' households. See Joseph Blenkinsopp, "The Family in First Temple Israel," in *Families in Ancient Israel*, ed. Leo G. Perdue, Joseph Blenkinsopp, John J. Collins, and Carol Meyers (Louisville: Westminster John Knox, 1997), 59. Given this, widows were particularly vulnerable. See Westbrook, *Property and the Family*, 154–55.

24 Frymer-Kensky notes how Judah commands her to "live as a widow" and thereby "must stay bound to Judah or be subject to severe punishment, even death." Frymer-Kensky, *Reading the Women*, 268.

widower and even perhaps that he is eager for a sexual encounter, as seems clear from what happens next.[25]

Tamar learns that Judah is en route to Timnah to shear sheep and springs into action in Genesis 38:13–15:

> Tamar was told: "Your father-in-law is going up to Timnah to shear his sheep." She removed the clothes of her widowhood from upon her and wrapped herself in a veil. She sat at the entrance to Enaim which is on the road to Timnah for she saw that Shelah grew up and she was not given to him as a wife. Judah saw her and considered her to be a promiscuous woman for she covered her face.

Although Tamar is a passive recipient of information and the object of Judah's gaze, she is an active figure who takes hold of her own fate. She sees (ראתה) that Shelah is old enough to be married and understands that Judah is remiss in not marrying her to Shelah. Tamar removes her widow's garb and situates herself at Enaim.

This passage plays overtly with the motif of sight, suggesting that Tamar sees clearly while Judah does not. Judah certainly does not recognize who she really is and misidentifies her as a promiscuous woman. Also, Tamar's location—פתח עינים—can mean the entrance or opening of either eyes or springs.[26] Both possible translations are apt to the situation, although each highlights different themes and presents a different character as the narrative's focus. This ambiguity invites an equivocal reading that encompasses these differences, allowing them to coexist.

As Leuchter observes, springs evoke "mythic concepts not only of life and fertility but also of divinity and royalty."[27] If Tamar sits at the entrance of Enaim-Springs, she becomes a symbol of fertility that evokes the promise of the royal line that will extend from Judah through her. Judah becomes the focus of the story. He has something to gain from the encounter with Tamar at the entrance of the springs. If Tamar sits at the entrance of Enaim-Eyes, the focus of

---

25 Ibid., 269.
26 Leuchter describes the toponym as a "symbolic double entendre." Leuchter, "Genesis 38," 221.
27 Ibid.

the narrative is on Tamar and Judah's obligation to her. Her location at the opening of eyes demands that Judah open his eyes, recognize his duty toward her, and fulfill his obligation to perform
levirate marriage. Tamar has something to gain from this encounter. Notably, Judah's recognition is not immediate but comes at the
narrative's conclusion.

Many readers assume that Tamar hides her identity by veil-
ing herself in order to deceive Judah. Frymer-Kensky suggests that
Tamar adopts "an anti-recognition strategy" and "draws a veil across
Judah's eyes and prevents him from seeing her identity."[28] Yet it is
unclear if Tamar seeks to disguise her identity or if Judah fails to
recognize her. This distinction is significant when considering who
looks righteous and who looks powerful at this point in this narrative. The passage specifically notes how Tamar removes her widow's
garments and puts on a veil, which Judah assumes marks her as a
prostitute. The text does not specify Tamar's intention in putting on
the veil and, therefore, is open to multiple understandings. Frymer-
Kensky may be correct that Tamar intentionally disguises herself
and prevents Judah from recognizing her, although her objectives
are not explicit. Tamar's disguise could be the most effective way to
get what she wants. Her actions could be viewed negatively. Unconcerned with Judah's well-being, Tamar is willing to deceive him and
have him violate the prohibition of such a relationship to serve her
own interests. Alternatively, her disguise could be a way to protect Judah from being held responsible for engaging in a prohibited
sexual relationship. If Judah cannot recognize Tamar, he cannot be
held accountable for sleeping with his daughter-in-law. Seen in this
way, Tamar's deception serves Judah's interests, which may align
with her overall intent, the protection of Judah's line.

Another possibility is that Tamar does not wear a disguise at all.
Rather, she selects clothes that communicate a particular message
without necessarily shrouding her identity. Frymer-Kensky observes
how veils were associated with marriage more than with prostitu-
tion in the ancient world.[29] Given this, Tamar may be presenting
herself as a married woman to communicate to Judah her status
as Shelah's promised wife. She may even be presenting herself as

---

28 Frymer-Kensky, *Reading the Women*, 270.
29 Ibid.

a possible wife *for* Judah. Tamar's clothes may signal to Judah that she, like Judah, is ready for marriage.[30] In other words, she may have no intention of deceiving Judah at all. This reading is particularly logical if she sits at the opening of the eyes. It seems unlikely that Tamar intends to deceive Judah at this location. Since she speaks directly to Judah, it is also hard to imagine that she would not be recognized by her voice, despite a disguise.[31] In this reading, Tamar wants Judah to recognize who she is and his duty toward her.

But Judah fails to recognize Tamar and considers her a promiscuous woman, and he has no hesitation in approaching her for sex (Gen 38:16–19):

> He heads toward her on the road to Timnah and says: "Come let me have sex with you," for he did not know that she was his daughter-in-law. She said: "What will you give me for having sex with me?" He said: "I will send a goat from my flock." She said: "You must give a pledge until you send it." He said: "What is the pledge that I should give you?" She said: "Your seal, your cord, and the staff in your hand." He gave them to her, had sex with her, and she conceived for him. She got up and left. She removed her veil and dressed in her widow's clothes.

There can be no doubt that Judah wants sex and not marriage, despite Tamar's potential sartorial attempt to signal her desire for marriage. Judah's failure to identify Tamar demonstrates weakness, since the patriarch is so easily duped. It also demonstrates Judah's depravity. Judah clearly wants sex, and he is willing to sleep with a promiscuous woman (זונה) in order to have it.

The word זונה often is translated as "prostitute," although the root זנה has a more general meaning in the Bible and is used to

---

30 Judah is ready for sex, not necessarily marriage. A man has more liberty to distinguish between the two than a woman. For most women, sex should fall within the confines of marriage.

31 Dohyung Kim makes a similar observation: "It is highly inconceivable to me that Judah did not recognize Tamar, the daughter-in-law he had married to both his dead sons, if not in the disguise, at least when they spoke to make the contract." Dohyung Kim, "The Structure of Genesis 38: A Thematic Reading," *VT* 62 (2012): 556.

describe sexual promiscuity.[32] A זונה is a woman who transgresses the norms of appropriate sexual behavior but who does not necessarily receive payment. She could be an unmarried daughter who has sex with a man she is not betrothed to or a wife who has an adulterous affair.[33] Judah's assumption that Tamar is a promiscuous woman does not have to mean he assumes she is a prostitute, although he does offer to pay her. In fact, he could be correctly reading the veil as a sign of marriage and is willing to sleep with a married woman who seems to present herself as open to a sexual encounter. This would explain why he identifies Tamar in Genesis 38:22 as a קדשה, a cultic functionary. As Frymer-Kensky observes, there would be no condemnation of Judah for engaging a prostitute.[34] But there would be for sleeping with a married woman. This is a capital offense in biblical law.[35] His labeling her a cultic functionary and not a promiscuous woman (זונה) suggests that he is ashamed of his behavior.

Judah's willingness to sleep with a promiscuous married woman does not make him look particularly good, but his willingness to relinquish his seal, staff, and cord—the markers of his identity—makes him look even worse. Tamar asks for an object that would serve as a pledge (ערבון) until Judah could send a goat as payment. She demands that Judah leave with her the three objects often used transactionally throughout the ancient world as markers of identity. Johanna W. H. Bos equates these items to a "driver's license and passport."[36] These items have narrative importance at the story's end when Tamar uses them to identify the father of her child. Yet they are more than a narrative device. They are symbolic of what is at stake—Judah's identity—which is connected deeply to the continuation of his line. Judah's relinquishment of these items

---

32 See Phyllis Bird, "'To Play the Harlot': An Inquiry into an Old Testament Metaphor," in *Gender and Difference in Ancient Israel*, ed. Peggy L. Day (Minneapolis: Augsburg Fortress, 1989), 75–94.

33 Bird notes, "As a general term for extramarital sexual intercourse, *znh* is limited in its primary usage to female subjects, since it is only for women that marriage is the primary determinant of legal status and obligation." Ibid., 77.

34 Frymer-Kensky, *Reading the Women*, 270.

35 Deut 22:22.

36 Johanna W. H. Bos, "Out of the Shadows: Genesis 38; Judges 4:17–22; Ruth 3," *Semeia* 42 (1988): 46.

to Tamar has two possible symbolic implications. First, he is as willing to relinquish his identity in the moment as he was willing to relinquish his future identity by not marrying Shelah to Tamar and securing an heir. Second, he has put his future into Tamar's hands.

This second possible implication is less damning of Judah's character than the first. In this reading, Judah is not sacrificing his future. Rather, he is just not directing it. Perhaps on some level Judah recognizes Tamar and is willing to impregnate her, thereby defying the prohibition of having sex with one's daughter-in-law. Perhaps he thought there would be another way to handle Tamar's pregnancy that would not implicate him. As we see in the next chapter, King David tries to sidestep his paternity of Bathsheba's child.

This reading suggests that Judah is an active participant in Tamar's ruse. A similar reading could be offered to describe the behavior of the patriarch Isaac, who is deceived by his wife Rebecca into giving his blessing to his younger son Jacob in Genesis 27.[37] Viewed this way, both Judah and Isaac use female deception to protect their own needs while serving the overall needs of the biblical narrative. Isaac does not have to overtly deny his eldest, more beloved son his legitimate inheritance. Judah does not have to give his youngest son to a woman he views to be a black widow in order to continue his line. Instead, Isaac and Judah can use female deception to ensure the narrative progresses as it should. Both women then become tools of the patriarchs.

REHABILITATION AND RIGHTEOUSNESS

As Fuchs observes about Genesis 38, the birth of a male heir fulfills the telos of the narrative.[38] Yet Tamar's deception and action, although necessary and desired by Judah, may tarnish her character. Her character is forever associated with a necessary, undesired means to achieve a desired end—an act of desperation, or even depravity, as opposed to an act of virtue. In this way, her character serves Judah and reflects Judah's character. The question then arises of

---

37 I offer this interpretation in "Rebecca and Isaac," in *Gender-Play*, 136–60.
38 Fuchs, *Sexual Politics*, 71.

whether Judah's rehabilitation at the narrative's conclusion impacts Tamar. Tamar's character may grow and change along with Judah's. It is interesting that Tamar dresses again in her widow's garb after having sex with Judah. The contrast with Judah is notable. Judah easily sheds his identity as a widower and relinquishes his identity to Tamar. Tamar cannot so easily shed her identity, nor can she fully transcend her status. She resumes her widowhood—though one wonders if, having slept with Judah and effectively become his wife, her widow's costume is now the true disguise.

Whatever his shortcomings, Judah pays his debts, although not directly. He sends Hirah to deliver the goat on his behalf and, perhaps more importantly, to retrieve the items he used as collateral. Hirah is unable to locate the woman he identifies or misidentifies as a cultic functionary (קדשה). By identifying Tamar as a קדשה and not as a זונה, Hirah may be trying to protect Judah's reputation. Judah also may have told Hirah that he was with a קדשה out of embarrassment for having been with a promiscuous woman. If so, Hirah makes an honest mistake. In response to Hirah's failure to locate the woman, Judah decides to allow her to keep the items in her possession and not to continue searching for her. He explains that he does not want to be held in contempt (פן נהיה לבוז).

It is unclear what Judah is explicitly concerned about. He notably speaks in the first-person plural—lest *we* are held in contempt. This could suggest that Hirah is somehow complicit or that Judah's family's honor is at stake and not just his own. The concern also could suggest that the honor of Judah and of the promiscuous woman is at stake, which provides support for the reading that Judah knowingly had sex with a married promiscuous woman—a capital crime for both parties. By canceling the search, Judah does not draw attention to their crime.

Judah prefers that the woman keep the markers of his identity rather than that he continues to look for her. Time passes, and the story draws to a dramatic conclusion in Genesis 38:24–26:

> After three months, it was told to Judah; saying: Tamar, your daughter-in-law, indeed is pregnant through promiscuity. Judah said: "Bring her out so that she will be burned." She was brought out. She informed her father-in-law: "The man who these belong to, through him I have conceived." She said:

"Acknowledge! To whom do the seal, cord and staff belong?" Judah acknowledged and said: "She is more righteous than I because I did not give her to my son Shelah." He did not have sex with her again.

Judah and Tamar face each other in a showdown moment. Each exercises power over the other, and they overpower each other. Both experience a life-or-death moment. Each imposes a life-or-death moment on the other.

Judah accuses Tamar of conceiving through promiscuous behavior (הרה לזנונים). The return of the root זנה is striking and connects Tamar's actions and perhaps her character with the figure Judah met on the way to Timnah. Use of the root again may reveal that Judah knew or now knows that Tamar was the promiscuous woman—the זונה—he met on the road. He quickly sentences Tamar to death by fire. As I mentioned, adultery is a capital offense. Yet the Bible does not specify how the adulterers should die in Leviticus 20:10 or Deuteronomy 22:22. In Deuteronomy 22:21, a woman found guilty of not being a virgin upon marriage, and therefore considered adulterous, is stoned to death.

Interestingly, Leviticus 21:9 condemns a daughter of a priest to death by fire for promiscuity (תחל לזנות). Judah's choice of the form of punishment suggests that either he sees Tamar as a priestess[39] or that he picks an extreme form of punishment that works to wipe Tamar out completely, effectively removing her and any evidence of her from his life. Tamar manages to save her life and by doing so risks exposing Judah's actions and consequently risks condemning him to death. Adelman observes how Tamar avoids confrontation and "allows Judah either to deny the identity of the tokens or, conversely, to acknowledge them as his own."[40] Tamar's indirectness may communicate her vulnerability. Judah has authority in this moment. Tamar's life is in his hands, and therefore, she treads lightly. Yet her words "I have conceived [אנכי הרה]" have resonance in the greater biblical context and carry a clear and direct message that manifests Tamar's strength.

---

39 This supports Arbeitman's argument in "Tamar's Name," 347.
40 Adelman, *Female Ruse*, 78.

As I note in the next chapter, Bathsheba uses similar language (הרה אנכי) to inform King David that she is pregnant in 2 Samuel 11:5. Bathsheba, who is married to Uriah and pregnant with David's child, is in a life-or-death situation like Tamar. Both women are adulterers according to biblical law. Both women determine the fate of the Davidic line. In announcing their pregnancies, Tamar and Bathsheba do more than inform the fathers—they demand a response from them. Bathsheba's pronouncement causes David immediately to send for Uriah, who is on the battlefield. David's actions seem to be a response to Bathsheba as if Bathsheba's pronouncement "I am pregnant" was followed by a "so take care of this situation."[41]

Tamar's pronouncement could be a similar call to action. Read in this way, Tamar looks less vulnerable and more powerful. Her words become a demand for Judah to act. She commands Judah to recognize the objects and acknowledge his role as the father of her baby. Judah does what she commands and admits, "She is more righteous than I." Judah's admission (צדקה ממני) can be translated differently. As Frymer-Kensky notes, "'She is more righteous than I' is the most probable translation of ṣadeqah mimmennî," but there is "another possibility: 'She is righteous. It is from me.'"[42] Tamar's righteousness is not at issue with either translation. What is at issue is Judah's status in relation to Tamar. Judah may be saying that Tamar's righteousness outweighs his own, thereby acknowledging his own deficiencies. Alternatively, Judah may not be comparing himself to Tamar. Judah simply may be admitting that Tamar is righteous and correct and that he is the father of her child. His admission certainly clears Tamar's culpability and saves her life. But it also clears him of any wrongdoing. Since Judah withheld Shelah from her, neither Judah nor Tamar can be accused of adultery.[43]

---

41 Frymer-Kensky offers a similar reading: "Her stark words to David, the only words she says in the story, make it imperative that he do something. And so he takes action. He brings Uriah back to the palace to render a report on the war, and then sends him home for the night." Frymer-Kensky, *Reading the Women*, 149.

42 Ibid., 274.

43 Of course, there remains the issue of incest. Frymer-Kensky suggests that "the incest provision is suspended for the levirate" and that "the gossiping public would realize that a pregnancy by Judah validated Tamar's innocence." Ibid.

Both readings are possible. Yet how one understands this verse impacts how one answers the questions of whose interests are primarily served in the narrative and whether one views Judah or Tamar to be its focus. Indeed, Tamar's interests may be served by securing her rightful place in Judah's household. In doing so, she consequently secures Judah's patriline and is rewarded for her efforts with not one but two children. Her efforts prove that she is more righteous than Judah. Judah is willing to forfeit his identity for a moment of pleasure and does not work to secure his patriline and his family's identity for the future.

Alternatively, Judah's interests are being served by preserving his line. As I mentioned previously, Judah claims the children as his own in 1 Chronicles and not as the children of his dead sons. Genesis 38 can be about Judah's redemption in which Tamar plays a crucial role. Judah begins the narrative in disgrace, having just convinced his brothers to sell their brother Joseph into slavery. Tamar transforms him into a patriarch worthy of the monarchy. Her deception, which defies biblical law, is a means to an end—Judah's redemption. As the story's conclusion illustrates, Judah learns to love his patriline. His initial condemnation indicates that Judah is willing to kill Tamar. He stays his hand only after he realizes she is pregnant with his child. In other words, Judah is willing to kill Tamar but unwilling to kill *his* child. He has learned his lesson. He has learned the value of his patriline.

Conclusions

An equivocal reading of Genesis 38 captures the ambiguity within the narrative and the complexity of its characters. Judah is an important figure in the Bible with a difficult past. My reading of Genesis 38 captures this complexity and reveals the ways in which the narrative condemns and redeems Judah's character and the role Tamar plays in Judah's reformation. Contemporary feminist readers often celebrate biblical women who defy the Bible's patriarchs and patriarchy. Yet equivocal readers, who strive to balance generous and suspicious perspectives, recognize the Bible's complexity and perceive how these defiant women are essential to, but not necessarily celebrated within, their biblical contexts. We make room for interpretations that can elevate or circumscribe beloved characters and that question who the Bible celebrates.

My generous reading of Genesis 38 shows how Tamar outshines and outsmarts Judah, serving her own and the Bible's interests by securing Judah's patriline and her place within Judah's house. My suspicious reading recognizes how Tamar helps rehabilitate Judah, who becomes a noble patriarch worthy of siring the most significant patriline in the Bible. Both readings coexist and are supported by the biblical text. Thankfully, equivocal readers perceive and affirm alternative, even contradictory, readings that capture the Bible's innate depth and complexity.

CHAPTER SIX

BATHSHEBA, DAVID, AND SOLOMON

In chapter three, I argued that the book of Esther is an equivocal book with ambiguous heroes. Like Queen Esther, Queen Bathsheba is another ambiguous figure who may be viewed as a passive character used by the men in her life or as an active figure who uses the men in her life for her own gain. Although their stories are quite different, they begin in similar ways and share narrative features. Both Esther and Bathsheba attract kings and are brought into their palaces as sexual partners. Once in the palace, the women must confront their kings and make demands of them in response to existential threats. Both are successful, which suggests that biblical queens—or at least these biblical queens—come to wield influence and power.

Neither Esther nor Bathsheba begins her story in a position of power. Yet whereas Esther rises to power in the logical course of her narrative, Bathsheba's transition to power is starker. Bathsheba asserts her power overtly in the final moment of her narrative. Her story and consequently her character are often viewed as bifurcated. Readers find it difficult to reconcile the Bathsheba who David sees and sexually takes in 2 Samuel 11 with the Queen Bathsheba who demands that the dying David declare their son Solomon king in 1 Kings 1. In the first narrative, Bathsheba appears to be David's innocent victim. In the second, she seems to manifest political motives and manipulates David to achieve them. This bifurcation supports perceiving Bathsheba as an equivocal figure in an equivocal narrative.

Gale A. Yee considers literary ambiguity, "the narrative's quality of indeterminateness, its *equivocation*" (my emphasis), to be integral to the Bible's narrative technique. According to Yee, literary ambiguity invites "several interpretations at once, each supported by the text itself."[1] Yee asserts that the ambiguity in 2 Samuel 11 results from "ambiguity that exists between character action and motive" and that "motivational ambiguity sets off the whole chapter."[2]

The chapter opens with David remaining in Jerusalem while his troops go off to battle the Ammonites. It is unclear why David remains home. His decision reflects poorly on his character, as he seems more interested in indulging his sexual appetite than in supporting his troops. Bathsheba's motives are also unclear at the start of the narrative. Some readers suggest that with designs on the palace, Bathsheba presents herself before David, hoping to be noticed by him. If so, Bathsheba is not an innocent victim of David's voyeurism and unchecked sexual desire. She becomes a political operator, which is consistent with her character in the final narrative.

For Yee, literary ambiguity in the Bible serves the specific purpose of calling "forth a reader response in such a way that the moral purpose of the story is emphasized."[3] Yee argues, "The author's technique of leaving ambiguous motives which the readers especially desire to be crystal clear forces the readers to become more actively involved with the characters and the morality of their actions."[4] According to Yee, the literary ambiguity involves the reader in the narrative, working to align the reader with the story's moral conclusion. The final line of 2 Samuel 11 clearly condemns David's actions: "What David had done was wrong in the eyes of YHWH." The literary ambiguity that shapes the preceding narrative engages readers by asking them to draw moral conclusions throughout the narrative so that the final statement "confirms the readers' own

---

1 Gale A. Yee, "Fraught with Background: Literary Ambiguity in II Samuel 11," *Interpretation* 42 (1988): 240. Yee notes that ambiguity is achieved broadly in the following ways: "(1) in the tension between character action and motive, (2) by using the same words for different characters to produce character contrasts, and (3) in the variations between narration and dialogue." Ibid., 241.

2 Ibid., 242.

3 Ibid., 251.

4 Ibid.

moral intuitions regarding the story."[5] Indeed, agrees the reader
with the narrator, David has done wrong.

I agree with Yee in the ways she sees ambiguity related to characters' motives at work in the David and Bathsheba narrative and
with her understanding of how the Bible employs ambiguity as
a literary technique. Like Yee, I consider literary ambiguity to be a
central feature of biblical narrative. As I argue throughout this book,
literary ambiguity invites equivocal readings that offer multiple
ways of understanding biblical narratives. Through the use of literary ambiguity, the Bible intentionally engages readers and invites
these multiple interpretations. I differ from Yee in that I do not
think literary ambiguity helps readers draw one moral conclusion.
Instead, I contend that the Bible embraces inconsistent ideologies
and multiple meanings. The Bible is intentionally polyvalent—even
when dealing with moral issues. As I argue in the previous chapter, the Bible may condone or condemn Tamar's defiance of the
prohibition against having sex with her father-in-law. Genesis 38
intentionally allows for both perspectives.

The Bible does condemn David for his actions in 2 Samuel 11.
That is clear. What remains unclear is the extent of the condemnation and what precisely David is condemned for. It could be rape,
adultery, or murder. Also, it is unclear whether the guilt extends
beyond David in this narrative to include Bathsheba. An equivocal
reading allows for ambiguity in the Bible's intent and meaning. It
does not enable one meaning or moral lesson to be derived from a
story, as Yee suggests. In fact, the literary ambiguity integral to the
David and Bathsheba narrative ensures that there is more than one
moral to this story and that culpability can be shared. The story
condemns unchecked sexual appetite, adultery, and murder and
suggests that David and Bathsheba share responsibility in Uriah's
death, although not equally.

My equivocal reading of the Bathsheba and David story recognizes its ambiguity but argues particularly for a consistency of
Bathsheba's character and for a narrative arc in her story. I do not
see Bathsheba's character or story as bifurcated. Initially, Bathsheba
is David's victim, but she does not remain a passive figure even in
this first narrative. Instead, Bathsheba responds powerfully to her

---

5 Ibid.

situation, propels the narrative forward, and changes the course of history, as is abundantly clear in the final narrative. Although I see Bathsheba's vulnerability throughout her story, I consider her to be a powerful figure. In fact, I perceive Bathsheba to be among the most significant and powerful biblical figures. She secures and strengthens David's dynasty by ensuring that her son Solomon is heir to the throne. Notably, Bathsheba is a biblical mother whose story extends beyond the conception and birth of her child.

An equivocal reading of David and Bathsheba's story reveals the complexities of Bathsheba's character and motives, allowing her to be tragic and triumphant—vulnerable and powerful. In my equivocal reading, Bathsheba is motivated by self-preservation and revenge more than by greed and ambition—though these remain possible motives as well. Bathsheba's actions, I argue, offer a critique of David's yet also can be critiqued. In short, an equivocal reading reveals Bathsheba to be a complex figure with great impact. Like Hannah and Tamar, Bathsheba protects her own interests while ensuring that the Bible's interests are met.

Ambiguous Biblical Queens

In general, biblical queens are ambiguous figures. Relatively few come into narrative focus. Those who do can have significant roles, such as Queens Esther, Bathsheba, Jezebel, and Athaliah and the Queen of Sheba. Although these queens save nations, establish dynasties, and command great wealth, it is unclear whether their impact results directly from their position as queen. Scholars debate whether queens, particularly queen mothers who birth future kings, held official positions of authority.

Susan Ackerman argues that Israelite queen mothers, like Canaanite queen mothers, wield political and religious power. Ackerman finds support in letters from Ugaritic kings to their mothers in which the kings pay "homage to the authority of the queen mother by bowing at her feet,"[6] as Solomon does when greeting Bathsheba in 1 Kings 2:19. Also, Ugaritic queen mothers influence

---

6 Susan Ackerman, *Warrior, Dancer, Seductress, Queen: Women in Judges and Biblical Israel* (New York: Doubleday, 1998), 134.

succession and "play a role in naming their husbands' heir," as Bathsheba does.[7] Ackerman also argues that Israelite and Canaanite queen mothers "had an official function within their cultures' religious communities," which was "to devote themselves to the cult of the mother goddess Asherah."[8] According to Ackerman, if Judean royal ideology perceives YHWH to be "the metaphorical father of the king," as Psalms 2:7 and 72:1 suggest, then it is reasonable to assume that Asherah, the female consort of YHWH, was the "monarch's surrogate mother" and that the queen mother "would be perceived as the earthly counterpart of Asherah" and "might even be considered the human representative of Asherah."[9]

Nancy R. Bowen challenges Ackerman's conclusion that the queen mother held a position of political and religious authority.[10] Bowen suggests that the term *gebira*, often translated, as Ackerman does, to be "queen mother," should be translated as "Great lady" or "Principal lady" and does not *necessarily* communicate official political or religious status or even her precise relationship to the king. Who she is and the role she serves is ambiguous. The *gebira* could be the king's mother but also his wife or even grandmother. The Great lady, Bowen writes, "appears to be the one who held the principal rank among all the royal women," although her "power and influence are circumscribed by the king, who can strip her of her rank."[11]

---

7 Ibid., 136. Ackerman writes, "Commentators generally agree that the kinds of economic and political power ascribed to Canaanite and Israelite queen mothers have their roots in Hittite culture (c. 2000–1180 B.C.E.), where the queen mother or *tawananna* had significant responsibilities in managing the economic and political affairs of the king's court." Ibid., 138.

8 Ibid., 139.

9 Ibid., 154. How normative Asherah worship was in ancient Israel is debated by scholars. The Bible directly links Asherah worship with Queen Maacah in 1 Kgs 15:13 and with Queen Jezebel in 1 Kgs 18:19. Kings Asa, Hezekiah, and Josiah work to wipe out Asherah worship from the Jerusalem temple. From this Ackerman concludes, "These multiple texts suggest that it was the norm in the southern kingdom in the ninth century, the eighth century, and the seventh century to worship both Yahweh and Asherah in the state temple in Jerusalem. The zeal of the reformer kings, Asa, Hezekiah, and Josiah, to remove the Asherah cult was the exception." Susan Ackerman, "The Queen Mother and the Cult in Ancient Israel," *JBL* 112, no. 3 (1993): 391.

10 Nancy R. Bowen, "The Quest for the Historical Gebira," *CBQ* 64 (2001): 602.

11 Ibid., 618.

Bathsheba does not receive the title of *gebira* even though, as Solomon's mother, she is the queen mother. Although her religious significance is unknown, her political significance is clear in the narrative. Bathsheba secures the throne for her son Solomon by having David swear that Solomon would succeed him and by removing Solomon's rival, Adonijah. In this way, Bathsheba proves herself to be a Great lady. Her power, I argue, is not inherent in her position as queen. Instead, it comes from her character and the experiences she endures. Bathsheba does not assume power when she becomes queen; she asserts power even before becoming queen in response to the difficulties she faced. Bathsheba's power is born from hardship and vulnerability and not from position and status.

An Equivocal Reading of 2 Samuel 11–12: Bathsheba as Uriah's Wife

As many readers note, Bathsheba enters the narrative as an object of David's gaze. At home one evening in the palace while his troops are battling the Ammonites, David strolls on his rooftop and sees Bathsheba, a beautiful woman, bathing on her rooftop. David then acts on his apparent desire for Bathsheba in 2 Samuel 11:3–4:

> David sent to inquire after the woman and said: "Is this not Bathsheba, daughter of Eliam, wife of Uriah the Hittite?" David sent messengers and he took her. She came to him. He lay with her. She purified herself from her impurity and returned to her house.

David's motives in this passage are clear. He wants to have sex with Bathsheba. What is less clear is whether the Bible is critical of his actions and whether it considers them to be criminal. It is possible that the Bible is critical of David but does not consider his actions to be criminal.

Contemporary readers are more likely to condemn David's actions and consider them to be criminal. These readers debate whether David is guilty of rape as understood today. Alexander Izuchukwu Abasili recognizes "the cultural and contextual differences between the Hebrew biblical conception of sexual-coercion and the contemporary understanding of 'rape.'"[12] Abasili notes, "In the Hebrew bible, the concept of coerced sexual relationships is not as wide and all embracing as the contemporary conception of rape. The Hebrew bible does not emphasize the role of psychological, emotional and political coercion in rape, instead it stresses the vital role of physical force or violence."[13] According to Abasili, physical force must be evident to identify a rape in the Bible as it is in passages such as Judges 19 and 2 Samuel 13. Bathsheba may feel coerced by the king, but she is not physically forced by him and, therefore, cannot be considered raped by him. For Abasili, the fact that Bathsheba comes to David indicates a degree of willingness on her part and consequently some amount of culpability in what follows.[14]

George G. Nicol makes a similar argument but goes one step further: Bathsheba not only is willing to engage in adultery with David; she is a "clever and resourceful woman who in marrying David evidently achieves her goal."[15] Nicol acknowledges the ambiguity of the passage[16] but suggests the possible reading that Bathsheba presents herself to David when bathing on her roof. By bathing on the roof in David's line of sight, Bathsheba is being "deliberately provocative"[17] and, therefore, is not only complicit in but actually initiates the events that follow.

Like Nicol, Exum recognizes the ambiguity in the passage, although she offers a very different reading from Nicol. She distinguishes between "rape that is recounted in a narrative" and "rape that takes place by means of a narrative."[18] In Exum's reading, the "rape of Bathsheba is something that takes place not so much in the story as by means of the story . . . in depriving her of voice and

---

12 Alexander Izuchukwu Abasili, "Was It Rape? The David and Bathsheba Pericope Re-examined," *VT* 61 (2011): 4.

13 Ibid., 4–5.

14 Ibid., 11.

15 George G. Nicol, "The Alleged Rape of Bathsheba: Some Observations on Ambiguity in Biblical Narrative," *JSOT* 73 (1997): 53.

16 In support of equivocal readings, Nicol writes, "Clearly the presence of (so much) ambiguity admits to discussion the possibility of more than one reading; other possible readings might well be constructed and so far as they are coherent and consistent must be permitted to stand alongside the one I have advanced here." Ibid.

17 Ibid., 44.

18 Exum, *Fragmented Women*, 170.

in portraying her in an ambiguous light that leaves her vulnerable, not simply to assault by characters in the story but also by later commentators on the story."[19] By not including Bathsheba's perspective, the Bible denies her any subjectivity. Readers cannot know what Bathsheba thinks or feels when David takes her sexually. For Exum, the "denial of subjectivity is an important factor in rape, where the victim is objectified and, indeed, the aim is to destroy her subjectivity."[20] In Exum's reading, David may or may not have raped Bathsheba, but the text does by objectifying Bathsheba, and readers—who are placed in the position of "voyeurs"—are forced to participate.[21]

In contrast to Exum, I do not think that Bathsheba is completely objectified in or by the narrative. I agree with Exum that Bathsheba appears initially in the narrative as an object of David's desire and that readers first perceive Bathsheba through David's objectifying gaze. Yet like Abasili and Nicol, I perceive agency in Bathsheba's coming to David and in her response after he takes her sexually. Like Nicol, I perceive Bathsheba to be a clever and resourceful woman who responds to her circumstances and protects her interests. In my reading, though, Bathsheba does not have designs on the throne. Rather, she wants to stay alive, and staying alive means eliminating Uriah and becoming David's queen. Her actions have enormous narrative consequences. Not only do they ensure the birth of Solomon, David's heir; they also serve to critique David's actions by demonstrating and taking advantage of his weaknesses.

As I note, many readers recognize that 2 Samuel 11 opens with ambiguity. David's motivation for remaining in Jerusalem while his army goes forth in battle is unstated and potentially damning for this warrior king, who seems more interested in satisfying his own desires than protecting his kingdom.[22] In this way, David is not

---

19 Ibid., 171.

20 Ibid., 173.

21 Ibid., 174.

22 Yee notes the ambiguity and writes, "The juxtaposition would set the stage for the story of a king having an affair with a woman whose husband was away fighting the king's battles." Yee, "Fraught with Background," 243. In contrast, Moshe Garsiel argues, "Several kings had made peace with David, and Ammon was left isolated, so that its surrender was not of great moment to Israel's future. The war also

unlike his ancestor Judah, who satisfies his sexual desires instead of fulfilling his duties as patriarch. David's presence in the palace may indicate callousness or hedonism and, therefore, works to debase his character from the start of the narrative; it also would be unexpected to Bathsheba. This is the time when kings go forth in battle. Bathsheba's husband, Uriah, has gone to fight with David's army. It is logical for Bathsheba to assume that David has gone to battle as well, and therefore, her bathing on the rooftop is not a means to attract David's attention.

There is no reason given for Bathsheba's bath. Some readers assume she is ritually purifying herself after having her period and suggest that her bath communicates to David that she is pure and fertile.[23] This assumption is unfounded. As I noted, Bathsheba would have had no reason to assume that David was home and not in battle. In fact, it is more logical for Bathsheba to assume that David was not at home and that he, along with all the men of Israel,[24] went to battle, permitting Bathsheba to bathe in private without being subjected to the male gaze. Her bath, therefore, is not part of a strategy to make the king notice her and invite her into the palace. Also, as I mention later, there is no reason to assume she is bathing ritually after menstruating.

For both David and Bathsheba, their encounter is at first by chance. David does not recognize the woman who is bathing and inquires who she is. Yet when David sends for Bathsheba, he knows precisely who she is. He knows her name, who her father is, and most importantly who her husband is. In other words, David takes Bathsheba into the palace with the intent to commit adultery. He knows what he is doing and what is at stake. Second Samuel 11:4 describes their sexual encounter:

> David sent messengers and he took her. She came to him. He lay with her. She purified herself from her impurity and returned home.

---

involved a lengthy siege of the Ammonite cities. Hence, David's preferring to stay in Jerusalem does not imply a failure in his royal duty." Moshe Garsiel, "The Story of David and Bathsheba: A Different Approach," *CBQ* 55 (1993): 250.

23 See Caryn Tamber-Rosenau, "Biblical Bathing Beauties and the Manipulation of the Male Gaze," *JFSR* 33, no. 2 (2017): 59–60.

24 2 Sam 11:1 records that "all Israel" went with Yoab and his officers into battle.

David performs three actions in this verse. He sends for, takes, and lies with Bathsheba. Likewise, Bathsheba performs three actions in this sentence. She comes, purifies herself, and returns home. Notably, the text records that Bathsheba comes to David before it relates that he lies with her. As Abasili observes, this "noteworthy" insertion "suggests that Bathsheba is not carried by force to the king; she willingly goes to answer the king's call."[25]

Jennifer Andruska similarly notes how the inclusion of the phrase "she came to him" "interrupts the rush through five verbal clauses" and can indicate Bathsheba's compliance either as a "willing participant" or as a subordinate.[26] Andruska also notes that the phrase is missing from the Septuagint, which may indicate it is not original to the text or that it was omitted "to emphasize that it was not consensual."[27]

In contrast to Exum's claim that the narrative denies access to Bathsheba's point of view, I contend that Bathsheba's autonomous actions do provide limited access. In my reading, Bathsheba's actions transform her from object to subject and suggest that she is complicit to a degree in what happens, though her motives remain unknown. Given the power differential between David and Bathsheba, the question of whether Bathsheba could have refused the king's call must be asked.[28] Yet even if Bathsheba had no choice but to comply, the text's pivot to her makes Bathsheba the focus and gives her some autonomy. She comes to him, perhaps motivated by a genuine desire to serve her king or perhaps motivated by the fear of what would happen should she refuse. Either way, Bathsheba's action disrupts David's acts of sexual aggression and takes some control from him.

Bathsheba continues to act after David lies with her. The disjunctive phrase "she purified herself from her impurity" is challenging. Some readers consider this phrase to be parenthetical and connect it to the initial mention of Bathsheba bathing, as the NJPSV translation reflects:

---

25 Abasili, "Was It Rape?," 11.

26 Jennifer Andruska, "'Rape' in the Syntax of 2 Samuel 11:4," *ZAW* 129, no. 1 (2017): 103.

27 Ibid., 104.

28 Exum writes, "The king sends for a subject and she obeys. His position of power gives him an advantage: he 'takes.'" Exum, *Fragmented Women*, 172–73.

> David sent messengers to fetch her; she came to him and he lay
> with her—she had just purified herself after her period—and
> she went back home.[29]

This reading could support the notion that Bathsheba was communicating her fertility and availability to David.

My reading perceives Bathsheba's purification as an action
that occurs after she has sex with David. There is no reason to
assume that Bathsheba's initial bath had anything to do with
menstruation. The laws related to menstruation appear in Leviticus 15, which details the rituals required of an individual who
experiences the emission of certain bodily fluids to purify themselves. The rituals vary depending on the bodily fluid and include
bathing, washing clothes, prescribed time, and sacrifices. Unlike
rabbinic law, biblical law surprisingly does not mandate bathing
as part of the ritual of purification after menstruation, although
for generations commentators have assumed bathing is implied
but not mentioned. Yet Leviticus 15 specifically mentions bathing
throughout the chapter and does not seem to imply bathing for
any other ritual impurity mentioned. In my view, it simply is not
logical that bathing would be implied but not mentioned for the
menstruant when it is mentioned for someone who comes in contact with her bedding.[30]

Nicole Ruane argues that in the Bible, bathing as a purification
ritual is connected to an individual's status and that women generally are not required to bathe in order to purify themselves. Leviticus 15:18, which mandates bathing for both a man and a woman
after they have had sex, is a notable exception. Ruane explains this
exception as reflecting the fact that the woman has absorbed the
man's impurity through his semen and, therefore, must purify herself as a man would.[31] One could say that through sex, a woman
has contracted maleness. Given this, there is more reason to assume
that Bathsheba purifies herself after having sex with David than
after menstruating.

---

29 2 Sam 11:4 NJPSV.

30 Lev 15:21.

31 Nicole J. Ruane, "Bathing, Status and Gender in Priestly Ritual," in Rooke, *Question of Sex?*, 66–81.

I contend that the disjunctive phrasing serves to emphasize her action and its significance. Bathsheba purifies herself *after* having sex with David but *before* she returns home. By doing so, she communicates publicly that she has had sex with David, thereby protecting herself. Should she become pregnant, as she does, everyone would know who the father is and presumably would hold her less accountable. David did not hide his interest in Bathsheba and sent messengers to bring her to the palace. Bathsheba may not speak up until this point, as Alice Bach observes, but she communicates loudly through body language.[32] Since adultery is a capital crime in the Hebrew Bible,[33] Bathsheba's actions are intentional and essential to her survival. Once she discovers she is pregnant, Bathsheba speaks in 2 Samuel 11:5–6:

> The woman conceived and sent word to David. She said: "I am pregnant." David sent word to Joab: "Send Uriah the Hittite to me." Joab sent Uriah to David.

For Bach, Bathsheba's simple statement describes her "function in the story." Bach observes that the narrative "does not provide any details of her state of mind" and consequently "has eliminated a direct route of sympathy between the reader and the female character."[34]

I disagree strongly with Bach's reading of this moment. Bathsheba speaks simply, but her words are carefully crafted and carry enormous weight. First, it is significant that Bathsheba informs David of her pregnancy, which, as Nicol observes, involves "him fully in her predicament" and communicates to him "that she will not suffer the consequences of their adultery silently or alone, and that she looks to him to solve their problems."[35] I disagree slightly with Nicol in that I do not think Bathsheba is asking David to solve their problems. By informing David that she is pregnant, Bathsheba knowingly is initiating a chain of events and is helping solve their problem. She is also holding David accountable.

---

32 Bach, *Women, Seduction, and Betrayal*, 135.
33 Lev 20:10.
34 Bach, *Women, Seduction, and Betrayal*, 135.
35 Nicol, "Alleged Rape of Bathsheba," 50.

Bathsheba's communication to David is anything but a simple statement of fact that captures her function in the story. In fact, Bathsheba's purpose in this narrative is not to have a child. It may become her purpose as her story unfolds, but not at this moment and not with this child.

Bathsheba's admission bears enormous consequences that she may or may not be aware of. She may hope that David claims the child as his and claims her as his wife without endangering Uriah's life. But she also may think that the only way David could claim her would be to kill Uriah. She may be willing to kill her husband to save her own and her child's life. She also may desire David and the throne at whatever cost. As I noted previously, Bathsheba's motives are ambiguous. The ambiguity allows for complexity. Bathsheba may have more than one motive for informing David of her pregnancy. Whatever her motives, Bathsheba's communication initiates deadly events. It also offers a subtle critique of David's actions. As I observe in the previous chapter, Bathsheba's words echo Tamar's words to Judah in Genesis 38:25. When Tamar, pregnant with Judah's child, is brought to be burned for adultery, she produces Judah's seal, cord, and staff and declares, "The man who these belong to, through him I have conceived."

In both stories, the phrase "I have conceived" works to ensure that the father in question takes responsibility for the pregnancy and that the mother does not die for her crime. Judah takes responsibility, claims the child, and admits that Tamar is more righteous than he is. Judah's admission, as I suggest, is key to his redemption as a character, enabling him to become worthy of siring the royal line. In contrast to Judah, David does not respond directly to Bathsheba. He does not declare her to be righteous, let alone more righteous than he is. Instead, he sends for Uriah and initiates a plan that enables him to deflect his responsibility as the father by having Uriah return home and sleep with Bathsheba so that Uriah would think he is the child's father. Unsurprisingly, Judah is rewarded with the birth of twins while David's son dies prematurely. Bathsheba's announcement conjures the Judah and Tamar story and invites a critique of David in comparison. David is no Judah.

And Uriah is no David. Unlike David, Uriah refuses to have sex when a battle is raging. With his initial plan thwarted, David orders Joab to have Uriah killed in battle. David is now guilty of adultery and murder. He also now is free to marry Bathsheba, as 2 Samuel 11:26–27 relates:

> When Uriah's wife heard that her husband Uriah was dead, she mourned her husband. Mourning passed and David sent and gathered her up to his home. She became his wife and bore him a son.

Referring to Bathsheba as Uriah's wife offers another critique of David, by making it clear that Bathsheba belonged to Uriah and not to David. Various interpreters note how this emphasis implies David's culpability and Bathsheba's victimhood. Garsiel comments on how the title "Uriah's wife" is "expressive of fidelity to her husband even after his death" and supports viewing Bathsheba as "a tragic figure involuntarily caught up in events."[36] Similarly, Bach wonders if "in lamenting for her husband, she is lamenting her own helplessness" and asks, "Is what the narrator calls mourning for her husband, perhaps lamenting for her own female destiny?"[37]

I agree that Bathsheba could not refuse David's sexual advances, and it would be fair to call her a victim at the beginning of the narrative. I also agree that Bathsheba's mourning at the end of the narrative condemns David. Yet I disagree that it communicates her helplessness. I do not think that she laments her own helplessness or her female destiny. Rather, I understand her mourning to be another proactive use of body language intended to protect Bathsheba while condemning David. Mourning was a physical act in ancient Israel, involving weeping, cutting hair, and wearing dust and sackcloth.[38] Through these gestures, mourners communicated their sorrow and distress. Jeremiah 9:16–20 describes professional female mourners who sing dirges and weep publicly. I argue that Bathsheba engages in mourning activities as an intentional and public display designed to communicate her distress and to protect herself.[39]

---

36 Garsiel, "David and Bathsheba," 256.

37 Bach, *Women, Seduction, and Betrayal*, 136.

38 Josh 7:6; Jer 16:6; Ezek 24:16–17.

39 Her behavior resembles Mordecai's in Esth 4. Both Mordecai and Bathsheba mourn to communicate their emotional distress and to protect themselves.

Just as Bathsheba bathes to communicate publicly that she had sex with David, she mourns her husband publicly to communicate that she loved him, belonged to him, and did not want to have sex with David. Bathsheba may have been helpless to refuse David's sexual advances, but her mourning is not an act of helplessness. It is an act of communication and self-protection. After the mourning period passes, David sends for Bathsheba again and welcomes her into his house as his wife before their child is born. With Uriah dead and Bathsheba his legitimate wife, it would seem that David could move forward in his life and narrative. However, the final verse of chapter 11 declares, "What David did was bad in the eyes of YHWH." Although God clearly condemns David, this may be the most ambiguous line in the narrative. It does not specify what God condemns David for. It could be adultery, murder, or even the failure to claim responsibility for the adultery and murder.

The confrontation between David and the prophet Nathan in 2 Samuel 12 provides clarity. Nathan tells David a parable about a rich man who callously takes a poor man's beloved lamb. He equates the rich man to David and unpacks the parable. God gave David the throne, property, wives, and wealth, and yet that was not enough. Like the rich man in the parable, David wanted more and took what he wanted from a man who had less. It appears that David's essential crimes are greed and acting on his insatiable desires by taking Bathsheba, as 2 Samuel 12:10 conveys: "The sword will never turn from your house because you spurned me and took Uriah the Hittite's wife to be your wife." As further punishment, David's house will be divided and his wives will be violated. Also, David and Bathsheba's first child dies.

The death of their child could be viewed as a mutual punishment that Bathsheba must suffer along with David, suggesting that Bathsheba bears some degree of culpability. As I mention, Bathsheba informs David she is pregnant with the awareness that he must act on this information. She even may have expected him or wanted him to kill Uriah. In my reading, this makes Bathsheba culpable to a degree for Uriah's death. Abasili makes a similar point, although he views her culpability as related to the sexual act itself and her designs on the palace, which I do not. Abasili observes how "David gets a greater portion of the punishment for his dominant and commanding role in the sexual transgression" and that Bath-sheba's "minimal punishment" implies less guilt.[40]

An Equivocal Reading of 1 Kings 1–2: Bathsheba as Solomon's Mother

After the child's death, David comforts Bathsheba by having sex with her. They conceive another child whom Bathsheba names Solomon. God loves this child, as the text and his name indicate.[41] I suggest that this child not only comforts Bathsheba; he redeems her. Whatever culpability she bore for Uriah's death disappears with the birth of this child. Bathsheba's punishment ends. This is not so for David, whose punishment continues after Solomon's birth. It is notable that Bathsheba names Solomon and not David. Although other biblical mothers name their sons, I argue that Bathsheba's naming Solomon and her recognition that he is blessed indicate a bond between Bathsheba and Solomon—an intimacy that connects mother and son that excludes David, who remains marked by sin.

Joyce Willis, Andrew Pleffer, and Stephen Llewelyn note that David refers to Solomon only once as his son in 1 Kings 1:33. Otherwise, Solomon is identified as Bathsheba's son. They question David's paternity and suggest that Solomon's birth announcement in 2 Samuel 12 "was introduced into the story to add legitimacy to Solomon's position."[42] In my reading, there is no reason to question whether David is Solomon's biological father to account for David's distance from Solomon. David distances himself from Solomon, Bathsheba's son, in order to distance himself from the sin he committed. He distances himself from the son of the woman who reminds him of his sin. As the story unfolds, it becomes evident that David is more aligned with his son Absalom, the son of Maacah,[43] than he is with Solomon. Solomon belongs to Bathsheba.

---

40 Abasili, "Was It Rape?," 12.

41 1 Sam 12:24–25.

42 Joyce Willis, Andrew Pleffer, and Stephen Llewelyn, "Conversation in the Succession Narrative of Solomon," *VT* 61 (2011): 138.

43 2 Sam 3:3.

Bathsheba's distance from David and her alignment with Solomon are abundantly clear in the succession narrative that concludes Bathsheba and David's story. As I mentioned previously, many readers perceive Bathsheba in this story as a dramatically different character than she is at the start of her narrative. Whereas Bathsheba only speaks to inform David she is pregnant in 2 Samuel 11, she finds her power and voice in 1 Kings 1–2 and makes history. Bach notes Bathsheba's dramatic transformation "from sexual object to matriarch," who is now seen and heard, and who no longer plays "a monoactive role in the narrative."[44]

Bach wonders if the years spent in David's court changed her. Although I recognize that Bathsheba has grown as a character, I argue that Bathsheba's growth is a direct result of her experience in 2 Samuel 11 and is consistent with her character in that narrative. In the succession narrative, we see a woman who is deferential but not afraid to confront authority. We also see a woman willing to kill in order to protect herself and secure her position. In these ways, the Bathsheba of the succession narrative is not so different from the Bathsheba of 2 Samuel 11. Not only do I see consistencies in character; I also view the succession narrative to be on a continuum with 2 Samuel 11. I support Exum's suggestion "that by taking advantage of David's apparent senility in order to obtain the throne for her son Solomon, Bathsheba gets her literary revenge against David for taking advantage of her."[45]

Like Bathsheba, David appears to undergo a dramatic transformation in the succession narrative, which opens with him as an impotent old man. As Exum describes, "The once lustful and virile monarch is now old and senile."[46] Perhaps the greatest irony of all is either David's inability to be intimate with or his disinterest in Abishag, the beautiful young woman who was brought to his bed to keep him warm. David's insatiable sexual appetite appears to have completely disappeared. The contrast between David and Bathsheba in the succession narrative is also stark. Whereas David appears diminished and vulnerable, Bathsheba appears larger and more powerful both in comparison to who she was in the earlier narrative and also in comparison to David.

---

44 Bach, *Women, Seduction, and Betrayal*, 142.

45 Exum, *Fragmented Women*, 200.

46 Ibid., 198.

David is at the end of his life, and his kingdom is in tumult. His son Adonijah has declared himself king with the support of the priest Abiathar but without the support of the priest Zadok or the prophet Nathan. Nathan asks Bathsheba to save her own life and the life of her son Solomon and approach David to say, "Did you not my lord, the king, swear to your maidservant and say 'Indeed, your son Solomon will rule after me and sit upon my throne'? Why then does Adonijah rule?"[47]

It is interesting to observe that Nathan appeals to Bathsheba's desire to protect herself and her son and not to a desire for the throne. This is consistent with my earlier reading that Bathsheba did not have designs on the throne in 2 Samuel 11. Self-preservation, and not ambition, motivates Bathsheba. Bathsheba agrees to Nathan's plan and speaks to David in 1 Kings 1:15–21:

> Bathsheba comes to the king in his chamber. The king is very old and Abishag the Shunammite attends to the king. Bathsheba bows before the king. The king says: "What do you want?" She says to him: "My lord, you swore to YHWH, your God and to your maidservant: 'Your son Solomon will rule after me and that he will sit on my throne.' Now, Adonijah rules and my lord the king does not know. He sacrifices many oxen, fatlings and sheep and invites all the king's sons and Abiathar the priest and Yoab the commander of the army, but Solomon your servant he does not invite. The eyes of all Israel are upon you, my lord king, to tell them who will sit upon my lord king's throne after him, for when my lord the king lies with his ancestors, I and my son Solomon will be seen as sinners."

Bathsheba's words to the king are masterful. Not only does she elaborate on what Nathan tells her to say; she changes Nathan's question to a statement "that allows David no room to disagree," as Exum notes.[48]

David swore not just to Bathsheba but to God—another rhetorical addition—that Solomon would be king. Bathsheba also

---

47 1 Kgs 1:13.
48 Exum, *Fragmented Women*, 199.

makes sure that David understands that her life and Solomon's life are at stake. She is exceedingly deferential to David, bowing before him and referring to him as "my lord the king." Doing so, she not only expresses respect for David but reminds him that he is still the king despite the fact that Adonijah has declared himself king and is behaving like a king in preparing a sacrificial feast. She makes it clear that all of Israel is looking to David, their true king, to proclaim his successor Solomon.

Before she finishes speaking to David, Nathan enters the room and affirms Bathsheba's words, although with interesting differences. Nathan does not say that David swore that Solomon would be king. Instead, he informs David that Adonijah is acting like a king, which must mean that David has declared him king. This difference avoids the potential falsehood of David's oath—there actually is no prior mention of such an oath—while at the same time highlighting Adonijah's insurrection. It is inconceivable to Nathan that Adonijah would behave like a king if David had not declared him to be so. The fact that Adonijah is doing this should be inconceivable to David as well and incite his ire. It is also interesting that Nathan mentions the threat to his own authority and not to the lives of Bathsheba and Solomon. This omission suggests that Nathan may in fact be using Bathsheba for his own personal gain.[49]

David is less moved by Nathan's appeal than by Bathsheba's. He dismisses Nathan and calls Bathsheba. In her presence, he swears that Solomon will become king. In response, she bows deferentially and expresses the hope that "my lord King David will live forever." Her words and action communicate her loyalty and respect for David while getting her what she wants—personal security for herself and her son.

David orders Solomon anointed as king. Afraid of Solomon's retaliation, Adonijah seeks refuge at the tabernacle's altar until Solomon swears not to kill him. Solomon indeed promises to preserve Adonijah's life if he acts with valor. Solomon orders Adonijah to go home. Yet Adonijah is not satisfied. He has one last move and he needs Bathsheba's help to make it. Adonijah approaches her with a request in 1 Kings 2:13–18:

---

49 Exum suggests similarly that Bathsheba may be a "pawn manipulated by Nathan." Exum, *Fragmented Women*, 199.

> Adonijah son of Haggith came to Bathsheba, Solomon's mother. She said: "Do you come in peace?" He said: "Peace." He said: "I have something to say to you." She said: "Speak." He said: "You know that the kingship was mine and that all of Israel wanted me to reign. But the kingship was removed and given to my brother in accordance with YHWH. Now I have one request I ask of you. Do not refuse me." She said to him: "Speak." He said: "Speak to Solomon the king for he will not refuse you that he should give me Abishag the Shunammite as a wife." Bathsheba said: "Good, I will speak on your behalf to the king."

Adonijah's request to marry Abishag is another attempt at insurrection. Although Abishag is not officially one of David's wives, her position in the court suggests that she cared for him and functioned as a nonsexual concubine.[50] Biblical sons who sleep with their fathers' wives or concubines do so as an act of rebellion. Reuben sleeps with his father Jacob's concubine Bilhah in Genesis 35:22 and is cursed for it by Jacob on his deathbed in Genesis 49:4.

Absalom sleeps with David's concubines in 2 Samuel 16:20–23 in a blatant act of rebellion. Adonijah's request to marry Abishag is a similar rebellion against David's authority and an attempt to regain the kingship. This is certainly how Solomon sees it, who states later that if Adonijah marries his father's concubine, being the older brother, he would have a legitimate claim to the throne. Although there is little ambiguity about Adonijah's motivation—he wants the kingship—there is some ambiguity about why he asks Bathsheba for assistance and even more ambiguity about why she agrees to help him. I contend that Adonijah appeals to a perceived rivalry between Abishag and Bathsheba and to Bathsheba's sense of poetic justice. Beautiful, young Abishag is intended to be David's companion. Mention of Abishag's presence attending the king when Bathsheba approaches him in 1 Kings 1:15 suggests that Abishag has replaced and displaced Bathsheba in David's court.

---

50 Abishag's status is unclear, as Willis, Pleffer, and Llewelyn note: "There is no indication within the text that Abishag was a concubine and as such a member of David's 'harem.'" Willis, Pleffer, and Llewelyn, "Succession Narrative," 141. In contrast, I argue that Abishag is intended to be David's concubine and therefore should be viewed as one, even though their relationship was not sexually consummated.

Adonijah may assume that Bathsheba would be eager to remove her rival Abishag from her son's court. Bathsheba may also want to symbolically take something away from David as an act of revenge for David's having taken her away from Uriah many years ago. Even though David is now dead, there may be some satisfaction for Bathsheba in doing so.

Bathsheba's willingness to assist Adonijah may indicate that Adonijah's calculations were correct and that Bathsheba is happy to remove Adonijah from David's and now Solomon's court. Yet there is another way to understand her willingness. She may fully understand the threat that Adonijah continues to pose to Solomon, especially should he marry Abishag. Bathsheba seeks to convey this threat to Solomon, anticipating fully how Solomon will respond in 1 Kings 2:19–23:

> Bathsheba went to King Solomon to speak to him about Adonijah. The king rose to greet her, bowed to her, and sat on his throne. He set up a throne for the queen mother and she sat to his right. She said: "I have one small request to ask you. Don't refuse me." The king said to her: "Ask, Mother, for I cannot refuse you." She said: "Let Abishag the Shunammite be given to Adonijah your brother as a wife." King Solomon responded and said to his mother: "Why do you request Abishag for Adonijah? You might as well ask for him the whole kingdom since he is my older brother and Abiathar the priest and Yoab son of Zeruiah are on his side." King Solomon swore by YHWH: "Thus will God do to me and even more if raising this matter does not cost Adonijah his life."

There can be no doubt that Bathsheba has weight in Solomon's court. Solomon's deferential greeting and the placement of Bathsheba's throne to his right conveys Bathsheba's status in the court and supports Ackerman's claim that queen mothers had official status in the Israelite court.[51] She certainly holds sway over Solomon, who says he can never refuse her.

---

51 Ackerman writes, "A comparison with Pss 80:18 (English 80:17) and 110:1, where the king is described as sitting at the right hand of God, even suggests that after

Bathsheba notably makes "one small request." Yet it is clear from Solomon's reaction that the request was anything but small. I suggest that Bathsheba knows the full weight of what she asks and downplays it perhaps to incite Solomon more or to distance herself from his reaction and its consequences.[52] Bathsheba behaves in this moment not unlike how she behaves in 2 Samuel 11 when she informs David that she is pregnant. In 2 Samuel 11, Bathsheba conveys information that she knows must be responded to and that could have lethal consequences for Uriah.

To be clear, Bathsheba is not directly responsible for Uriah's death. She does not demand the death or wield the sword that kills him. And she certainly is not responsible for the initial event that led up to Uriah's death. In my reading, that responsibility belongs to David alone. Yet she does bear some culpability for Uriah's death by informing David that she is pregnant. That is information that must be responded to and could sentence Uriah to death. Similarly, in 1 Kings 2, Bathsheba informs Solomon of Adonijah's request, fully aware of its implications and possible consequences. In both cases, Bathsheba is willing to have someone die in order to protect herself or someone close to her. She may have more official power in 1 Kings 2 than she has in 2 Samuel 11, but her instincts are consistent in both stories and are equally powerful and impactful.[53]

Conclusions

Queen Bathsheba is a consequential and powerful figure. Her story and character have complexity and, as I have argued, consistency.

---

the throne of the monarch himself, the chair assigned to Bathsheba is the place of highest honor on the royal dais." Ackerman, *Warrior, Dancer*, 137.

52 Willis, Pleffer, and Llewelyn write, "Bathsheba's role in the succession of Solomon has been established, as has her power within the palace, so she would have had full knowledge of Solomon's likely reaction. She knows it is no small request and so incites her son the king." Willis, Pleffer, and Llewelyn, "Succession Narrative," 142.

53 I view Bathsheba to be a powerful figure even though I recognize that she uses powerful men to wield her power. Exum views her differently and writes, "She is the quintessential manipulable woman, always acted upon by men—taken by David, used by Nathan, and imposed upon by Adonijah. Though she has voice this time around, there is a real question whether or not she has a voice of her own. Nathan's words, then Adonijah's, are placed in her mouth." Exum, *Fragmented Women*, 199.

She begins her narrative as a victim who is objectified and acted upon by a king. But she does not remain a victim for long. She responds immediately to her situation and works to protect herself. She uses the powers of body language and then her voice to ensure that David is implicated and assumes responsibility for his actions. Bathsheba's voice and power continue to grow in her narrative. She protects herself and her interests while changing the course of Israelite history by securing Solomon's throne and protecting it from a rival. Her final acts bring her story to an appropriate conclusion.

The wife of Uriah has become Solomon's mother—the queen mother. The woman who was sexually taken by King David secures the throne for her son and takes a seat beside him. Her growth as a character stands in stark relief to David's diminishment and serves to critique a king whose insatiable lust and abuse of power unleash havoc on his kingdom. David ends his life impotent and with a divided house.

Ambiguity is an essential part of Bathsheba's narrative, as it is throughout the Hebrew Bible. Ambiguity invites equivocal readings by preventing readers from drawing a singular meaning from a biblical narrative and by revealing the fullness of its characters. An equivocal reading of Bathsheba's story enables readers to perceive the complicated motives of its characters and to draw various conclusions about their intentions and actions. As a result, Bathsheba becomes a complex figure who is vulnerable and powerful, innocent and guilty, protective and vengeful. She is all these things, and perhaps much more.

UNEQUIVOCAL CONCLUSIONS FROM AN EQUIVOCAL READER

The rabbis describe the Hebrew Bible as having seventy faces[1] and encourage readers to "turn it over and over" to uncover all the meanings within it.[2] The rabbis understood that the Bible was open to multiple, if not infinite, interpretations. Yet recognizing the power of interpretation to uncover multiple meanings of biblical texts, as well as recognizing the limited ability of interpreters to uncover their real meaning, is different from claiming that the Bible is *designed* to have many meanings and to be interpreted.

As an equivocal reader, I cannot state with certainty what the Bible intends. In fact, I argue throughout this book that ambiguity is a core feature of biblical narrative that prevents readers from knowing what the Bible intends. I also argue that the Bible does not engage in narrative or theological fundamentalism. Biblical ambiguity, I assert, prevents simplistic, fundamentalist readings.

What I can say with certainty is that the Bible is a complicated text in both form and meaning and that its writers, editors, and its generations of readers have either contributed to or tolerated its complexity. I also can state unequivocally that the Bible's complexity is a great asset, if not its greatest asset, for its readers. The Bible's complexity has inspired generations of readers to interpret its stories, laws, and poetry and to discover new meanings that make this ancient text relevant to each generation.

---

1 Numbers Rabbah 13:15–16.
2 Pirkei Avot 5:22.

I also can state, albeit equivocally, that the pervasiveness of the Bible's complexity suggests intention. My equivocal readings, which hew close to the biblical text, reveal how complexity and ambiguity are integral to biblical narratives and characters. I consider the Bible's intricateness to be intentional at the compositional level and not to be a by-product of narrative transmission or sloppy editing. Of course, there is no way to prove this. I base my argument on the perception of a literary and theological coherence to the complexity that is evident in my equivocal readings.

Saul and David are figures with flaws and desires, whose complicatedness reflects Israel's complex relationship to its monarchy as does the intricate network formed between Hannah, Samuel, Saul, and the medium from En-dor. As outlaws, Potiphar's wife, Tamar, and the medium from En-dor are also complicated figures whose illegal behaviors propel Israel's story forward. Esther is a book with dueling saviors who reflect competing ideologies of assimilation and gender dynamics. Hannah, Tamar, and Bathsheba's stories complicate the Bible's typical maternal narrative by revealing maternal desires independent of the desire to produce a male heir to continue the patriline. Each of these mothers ensures the birth of an essential figure.

Certainly, the multifaceted nature of biblical characters and narratives has engaged generations of readers and is essential to ensuring the Bible's continued relevance. Perhaps the ancient writers and editors understood this attraction and adopted an opaque style to engage readers. Yet there is narrative precision and purpose to the complicated figures and narratives I have studied here, which suggests that their complexity is more than a rhetorical device to attract readers. The complexity contributes to the structure and meaning of the narratives. Also, this complexity is essential to the Bible's core concern—Israel's relationship with God. For this reason, above all else, I argue that the Bible intends to be complex. The Bible's complexity captures and conveys the intricate divine-human relationship and, more specifically, the complicated relationship between God and Israel. Complex characters and narratives make clear the extent and limits of human power, the extent and force of God's power, and most importantly what it means to serve God. It is my argument in *Equivocal Readings* that they are purposefully designed to do so.

Although humans take center stage, the Bible does not present heroes who are paradigms of righteousness to determine the course of Israel's history. Instead, it presents figures such as lucky captives, frightened and foolish kings, and determined queens and mothers whose stories reveal a central truth: God is the Bible's superhero and directing force. God determines the descent and ascent of Joseph, Saul, David, and Israel. God determines who is born to lead Israel. Certain designated humans are essential to the course God sets for Israel, but their personal qualities are not always laudable, and their success is not guaranteed. Sometimes they succeed by failing, like Saul, or like David and Bathsheba, they succeed through adultery and murder. In the Bible, human efforts—whether intentional or not, whether noble or not—ultimately come to serve God's plan for Israel. This does not mean that human beings are pawns in God's universe. Quite the contrary. The Bible recognizes the reality and power of human will that often clashes with divine will. This is evident in the Bible's first narrative, which is about human disobedience—a persistent theme and challenge throughout the Bible.

Despite the challenges posed by human will, divine will always prevails. The complexity of biblical characters and narratives portrays the determinative power of divine will by showing that regardless of efforts or appearances to the contrary, divine will always triumphs. In other words, complex characters and narratives prove God's strength. Esther may appear to be a reluctant participant in God's plan for Israel, but she is instead its champion and representative. Similarly, Judah cannot end his line, and David cannot designate the wrong successor. Efforts to do so must be thwarted to reveal fully God's power and plan.

Understanding how characteristic and narrative complexity are used to convey divine power and ensure God's plan for Israel is essential for understanding the roles women play in biblical narrative. Women frequently introduce complexity into biblical narratives. Given the Bible's patriarchal assumptions, women's independent desires and interests create challenges for the men who assume control over their lives—their fathers, brothers, and husbands—and create instability in their households. Potiphar's wife sexually desires Joseph. Hannah and Tamar go to great lengths to conceive children without the assistance of the patriarchs who control their lives. Esther and

Bathsheba overshadow their patriarchs to save their lives and support their people. Women's efforts to secure their desires and interests can involve unsanctioned behavior that defies societal norms. Potiphar's wife risks adultery. Tamar has sex with her father-in-law. The medium from En-dor conjures up a dead and reluctant prophet. Bathsheba's actions result in murder.

Although women often destabilize their narratives, God is by far the most disruptive and determinative force in the Bible, as Hannah's prayer relates in 1 Samuel 2:6–8:

> *YHWH causes death and gives life, brings down to Sheol and raises up.*
> *YHWH impoverishes and enriches, casts down and elevates—raising the*
> *poor from the dust, lifting the needy from the dung, to sit among the*
> *nobles, bestowing upon them a throne of glory, for the pillars of the earth*
> *belong to YHWH who has set the world upon them.*

This passage captures how God controls and potentially disrupts the social and natural orders, interrupting lives to engage with individuals and disrupting nature to engage with peoples. Complex characters, many of whom are women, provide opportunities for God to engage with human beings. Complex narratives provide evidence of God's engagement. Through these characters, we see how God directs and redirects the course of history, defying expectations and norms. By defying norms and odds, these characters and their stories demonstrate that God selects who will be born, who will die, and who will be designated as heirs and kings. Potiphar's wife brings Joseph, and consequently Israel, into Pharaoh's orbit and court. Hannah and Tamar birth the monarchy. The medium from En-dor dooms Israel's first king. Bathsheba secures the throne for Israel's third king. Esther saves her people. These complex women are essential actors in Israel's story by ensuring God's plan and securing Israel's destiny. They are game changers and destiny shifters. Their stories reveal that history, Israel's history, is not fixed. God intervenes to select patriarchs, matriarchs, peoples, and their kings. God can reject a king or a nation. Nothing is guaranteed.

The recognition of how female-centric narratives help portray God as a destabilizing force in an unstable world provides an explanation for why women, as destabilizing figures, appear prominently in the stories about the monarchy—one of the Bible's three dynastic institutions. Whether patriarchal, priestly, or royal, dynasties offer stability to society by enabling leadership to transfer to a designated heir who was born to lead the next generation. Dynasties *should* deter power struggles. Yet the origin stories of the three major dynasties in the Bible are about disruption and present God as a destabilizing and destructive force. They are told to communicate that God controls all of Israel's dynasties and can disrupt their assumed natural progression. Patriarch Abraham's firstborn Ishmael is not the designated heir despite the laws of primogeniture. God designates second-born Isaac, but even that designation is subject to divine whim when God orders Abraham to kill Isaac. Priest Aaron's sons Nadab and Abihu draw too close to God at the initiation of the cult and are suddenly killed. King Saul is removed in disgrace, and his children are denied the throne. The brutal removal of dynastic leaders and designated heirs at the start of their line sends a clear message. God determines who God relates to as patriarch, priest, or king.

Complicated and complicating women make this point clear in connection with the monarchy. Ruth (a complex character I discuss in *Dangerous Sisters of the Hebrew Bible*[3]), Hannah, Tamar, and Bathsheba take remarkable measures that upend narrative expectations and societal norms to have and protect their children. Their efforts result directly and, for Hannah, indirectly in establishing Israel's monarchy, particularly King David's line—Israel's most stable royal dynasty. The children of Hannah, Tamar, Bathsheba, and Ruth offer Israel stability, but the means through which they are born show the destabilizing power of women and of God. Surprisingly and miraculously, Israel's greatest king and strongest line descend from foreign women and incest. David's remarkable lineage reveals that he was not born to greatness or from greatness. Rather his humble birth narratives, along with his son Solomon's birth story and rise to power, show that God determines the success of David and his line.

---

3 Kalmanofsky, *Dangerous Sisters*, 157–74.

Women are powerful figures in these narratives. Hannah, Tamar, and Ruth go to extreme lengths to have children that only they seem to want. Once they become pregnant, Tamar and Bathsheba risk death to protect their unborn children. Bathsheba appears willing to kill to protect her sons. Esther risks her own life to save the life of her people. These women use their innate power to get what they want at great cost and against tremendous odds, but ultimately their power serves God and reveals God's power. Their narratives propel Israel's story forward in alliance with God's will and plan. For some feminist readers, this is an equivocal conclusion to draw because it relegates female power to serving God. Doing so may work to deny female power by seeing it only as an instrument of God's power. Some feminist readers may see the subjugation of female power, even when in service of God, to be the Bible's intention, reflecting its patriarchal agenda.

As an equivocal reader, I recognize this possibility, but I also relish the Bible's recognition of female power even if it is in service of God. Throughout my career, my work has convinced me that women indeed play a unique role in the Bible and that the Bible recognizes the power women have, related to their experience as women, and channels that power directly in service of God. This recognition continues to surprise, engage, and satisfy me as a reader.

Just as I did in my introduction, I now speak personally. As a Jewish feminist scholar, I am a complex reader of the Bible. Of course, all readers of the Bible are and have been complex, but my complexities as a feminist critical-religious reader create challenges for how I relate to the Bible and how I relate to my academic and religious communities. Critical readers of the Bible can perceive religious readers to be biased and unsophisticated. Religious readers can perceive critical readers to be irreverent naysayers. Feminist readers can perceive religious readers to be complicit in the Bible's patriarchal agenda. Religious readers can view feminist readers as agenda-driven eisegetes.

Given these tensions, my hyphenated identity is not always comfortable. It is challenging to integrate my religious identity with either of my critical or feminist identities. My Jewish identity shapes my relationship with the Bible, leading me to be a generous reader who seeks value in biblical laws and narratives despite the patriarchal values I recognize in them. Because of this, critical readers can accuse me justifiably of being biased and feminist readers of being complicit in the Bible's patriarchal agenda. Yet I have grown more comfortable with my complexities as a reader of the Bible after years of teaching and writing, and I have become grateful for them. In fact, I feel unequivocally that my unique complexity as a reader is my greatest asset. It has made me sensitive to the Bible's unique literary and theological complexity, helped me understand something essential about the Bible's power and meaning, and enabled me to develop a way of reading that feels organic to the Bible and vital to similar readers.

I wrote in my introduction that critical-religious readers strive to reveal what is timeless and time-bound in the Bible. Our critical perspectives help us see how the Bible reflects its ancient context while our religious perspectives urge us to look for values that transcend that context, remain relevant, and even enhance our lives. Many of us look for a timeless perspective on what it means to be human in a world that is not confined to human experience. I conclude by reflecting on what I consider lies at the heart of the Bible's timeless perspective. For me, a religious perspective perceives a reality apart from and greater than human experience and looks beyond the time-bound natural world to the timeless world of the supernatural. A religious perspective acknowledges a determinative force that structures, guides, and enhances all life and matter—whether animate or inanimate. In the Bible, this force is God. God embodies the timeless supernatural. God exists distinct from human beings and the natural world, manipulating and directing both. As Hannah's prayer expresses, God creates, guides, and enhances all life and matter. The pillars and the earth that sits upon them belong to God.

Although the whole world belongs to God, the history and contours of the relationship between God and Israel are the Bible's central focus. My equivocal readings, along with all my previous work, attest to the complexity of this live and passionate relationship. The complexity of God's relationship to Israel, and to its founders and leaders, is one of the things I value most about the Bible. It appeals to me religiously. I appreciate the intimacy of this relationship and what it conveys about the Bible's god. I appreciate the portrait of a relatable god that connects emotionally with human beings and that cares for human beings. I value the portrait of a god who directs and overpowers individuals and peoples but who also is emotionally vulnerable and who can be appealed to and swayed by human prayer. I even value the volatility of the Bible's god because it displays a deep personal connection.

God can be violent in the Bible, but God is not unjustifiably cruel. God does not enjoy causing pain. As Jeremiah 2:5–6 relates, God's violence against Israel, though severe and manifested in ways that are unacceptable, stems from God's love and from the feeling that Israel betrayed that love:

> Thus says YHWH: What wrong did your ancestors find in me that they distanced themselves from me and pursued nothingness? They did not say: Where is YHWH, the one who raised us from the land of Egypt and led us through the wilderness, through a land of desert and pits, through a land of drought and darkness, through a land no one has trespassed upon and in which no human has dwelt?

This passage expresses God's pain at Israel's rejection despite all the care that God has shown Israel. Although much of the Bible relates the acts that bind Israel to God, such as being liberated from Egypt and led through the wilderness, the Bible is mostly concerned with what it means for Israel to serve God. Rules of engagement comprise the legal portions of the Hebrew Bible, defining every aspect of Israel's social, cultic, and political reality in service of God. Biblical narratives offer different perspectives on divine service, revealing the tensions human beings feel and the difficulties they experience relating to God and submitting to God's will.

Just as I value the Bible's portrait of a relatable, emotionally vulnerable God, I value these narratives for revealing human frailty, resistance, and disobedience. I appreciate these stories for empowering humans and endowing them with independent desires, even when those independent desires conflict with God's plan. I appreciate these stories for showing how human efforts, whether intended to or not, ultimately can serve God. You do not have to be a righteous or willing person to serve God. You can have flaws and selfish motives and serve God. You can make mistakes and break laws and serve God. In other words, God relates to humans, not heroes in the Bible, and humans are complex beings.

Unequivocally, I am grateful for my complexities as a reader and feel deeply that critical-religious readers are crucial readers of the Bible. These readers provide essential insight into the construction of the Bible and its meaning and help the Bible remain a vibrant resource for faith communities. Critical-religious readers ensure not only that the Bible is studied as an ancient artifact but that it can be read as a living document in every generation. Critical-religious readers ensure that the Bible remains open to future generations by expanding the canon of interpretation with integrity as to who we are and, as my equivocal readings show, what the text is.

The Bible is time-bound and timeless. If we turn it over and over, we find old and new meanings. Our perspectives and complexities as readers reveal these meanings and enable us to see our own faces among the seventy faces of the Bible.

BIBLIOGRAPHY

Abasili, Alexander Izuchukwu. "Was It Rape? The David and Bathsheba Pericope Re-examined." *VT* 61 (2011): 1–15.

Ackerman, Susan. "The Queen Mother and the Cult in Ancient Israel." *JBL* 112, no. 3 (1993): 385–401.

———. *Warrior, Dancer, Seductress, Queen: Women in Judges and Biblical Israel*. New York: Doubleday, 1998.

Adelman, Rachel E. *The Female Ruse: Women's Deception and Divine Sanction in the Hebrew Bible*. Sheffield, UK: Sheffield Phoenix, 2015.

Alter, Robert. *The Art of Biblical Narrative*. New York: Basic Books, 1981.

Andruska, Jennifer. "'Rape' in the Syntax of 2 Samuel 11:4." *ZAW* 129, no. 1 (2017): 103–109.

Arbeitman, Yoël L. "Tamar's Name or Is It? (Gen 38)." *ZAW* 112 (2000): 341–355.

Bach, Alice. "Breaking Free of the Biblical Frame-Up: Uncovering the Woman in Genesis 39." In *A Feminist Companion to Genesis*, edited by Athalya Brenner, 318–342. Sheffield, UK: Sheffield Academic, 1998.

———. *Women, Seduction, and Betrayal in Biblical Narrative*. New York: Cambridge University Press, 1997.

Bakon, Shimon. "Subtleties in the Story of Joseph and Potiphar's Wife." *JBQ* 41, no. 3 (2013): 171–174.

Beal, Timothy K. *The Book of Hiding: Gender, Ethnicity, Annihilation, and Esther*. New York: Routledge, 1997.

Bekins, Peter. "Tamar and Joseph in Genesis 38 and 39." *JSOT* 40, no. 4 (2016): 375–397.

Bird, Phyllis. "'To Play the Harlot': An Inquiry into an Old Testament Metaphor." In *Gender and Difference in Ancient Israel*, edited by Peggy L. Day, 75–94. Minneapolis: Augsburg Fortress, 1989.

Blenkinsopp, Joseph. "The Family in First Temple Israel." In *Families in Ancient Israel*, edited by Leo G. Perdue, Joseph Blenkinsopp, John J. Collins, and Carol Meyers, 48–103. Louisville: Westminster John Knox, 1997.

———. "Saul and the Mistress of the Spirits (1 Samuel 28:3–25)." In *Sense and Sensitivity: Essays on Reading the Bible in Memory of Robert Carroll*, edited by Alastair G. Hunter and Phillip R. Davies, 49–62. New York: Sheffield Academic, 2002.

Bos, Johanna W. H. "Out of the Shadows: Genesis 38; Judges 4:17–22; Ruth 3." *Semeia* 42 (1988): 37–67.

Bowen, Nancy R. "The Quest for the Historical Gebira." *CBQ* 64 (2001): 597–618.

Brettler, Marc Zvi. "Incompatible Metaphors for YHWH in Isaiah 40–66." *JSOT* 78 (1998): 97–120.

Butting, Klara. "Esther: A New Interpretation of the Joseph Story in the Fight against Anti-Semitism and Sexism." In *Ruth and Esther: A Feminist Companion to the Bible (Second Series)*, edited by Athalya Brenner, 239–248. Sheffield, UK: Sheffield Academic, 1999.

Chaudhry, Ayesha S. "Naming Violence: Qur'anic Interpretation between Social Justice and Cultural Relativism." In *Sexual Violence and Sacred Texts*, edited by Amy Kalmanofsky, 95–124. Cambridge: Feminist Studies in Religion Books, 2017.

Coats, George W. "Widow's Rights: A Crux in the Structure of Genesis 38." *CBQ* 34 (1972): 461–466.

Conrad, Tony, and Tony Oursler. "Who Will Give Answer to the Call of My Voice? Sound in the Work of Tony Oursler." *Gray Room* 11 (Spring 2003): 44–57.

Davies, Eryl W. "Inheritance Rights and the Hebrew Levirate Marriage: Part 1." *VT* 31, no. 2 (1981): 138–144.

Day, Linda. *Esther*. Nashville: Abingdon, 2005.

———. *Three Faces of a Queen: Characterization in the Books of Esther*. Sheffield, UK: Sheffield Academic, 1995.

Dobbs-Allsopp, F. W. *Weep, O Daughter Zion: A Study of the City-Lament Genre in the Hebrew Bible*. BibOr 44. Rome: Pontifical Biblical Institute, 1993.

Ebeling, Jennie R. *Women's Lives in Biblical Times*. New York: T&T Clark, 2010.

Exum, J. Cheryl. "Feminist Criticism: Whose Interests Are Being Served?" In *Judges and Method: New Approaches in Biblical Studies Second Edition*, edited by Gale A. Yee, 65–89. Minneapolis: Fortress, 2007.

———. *Fragmented Women: Feminist (Sub)versions of Biblical Narratives.* Valley Forge, PA: Trinity International, 1993.

Foster, Julia A. "The Motherhood of God: The Use of *ḥyl* as God-Language in the Hebrew Scriptures." In *Uncovering Ancient Stones: Essays in Memory of H. Neil Richardson*, edited by Lewis M. Hopfe, 93–102. Winona Lake, IN: Eisenbrauns, 1994.

Fox, Michael V. *Character and Ideology in the Book of Esther.* 2nd ed. Grand Rapids, MI: Eerdmans, 2001.

Frymer-Kensky, Tikva. *In the Wake of the Goddesses: Women, Culture, and the Biblical Transformation of Pagan Myth.* New York: Free Press, 1992.

———. *Reading the Women of the Bible: A New Interpretation of Their Stories.* New York: Schocken, 2002.

Fuchs, Esther. *Sexual Politics in the Biblical Narrative: Reading the Hebrew Bible as a Woman.* Sheffield, UK: Sheffield Academic, 2000.

Garsiel, Moshe. "The Story of David and Bathsheba: A Different Approach." *CBQ* 55 (1993): 244–261.

Goitein, S. D. "Women as Creators of Biblical Genres." *Prooftexts* 8, no. 1 (1988): 1–33.

Hamori, Esther J. "The Prophet and the Necromancer: Women's Divination for Kings." *JBL* 132, no. 4 (2013): 827–843.

Hayes, Jeff. "Intentional Ambiguity in Ruth 4:5: Implications for Interpretation of *Ruth*." *JSOT* 41, no. 2 (2016): 159–182.

Hertzberg, Hans Wilhelm. *I & II Samuel.* Translated by J. S. Bowden. Philadelphia: Westminster, 1964.

Huddlestun, John R. "Divestiture, Deception, and Demotion: The Garment Motif in Genesis 37–39." *JSOT* 98 (2002): 47–62.

Kalmanofsky, Amy. *Dangerous Sisters of the Hebrew Bible.* Minneapolis: Fortress, 2014.

———. *Gender-Play in the Hebrew Bible: The Ways the Bible Challenges Its Gender Norms.* London: Routledge, 2017.

———. "The Monstrous Feminine in the Book of Jeremiah." In *Jeremiah (Dis)placed: New Directions in Writing/Reading Jeremiah*, edited by A. R. Pete Diamond and Louis Stulman, 190–208. New York: T&T Clark, 2011.

———. "Their Heart Cried Out to God: Gender and Prayer in the Book of Lamentations." In *A Question of Sex? Gender and Difference in the Hebrew Bible and Beyond*, edited by Deborah W. Rooke, 53–65. Sheffield, UK: Sheffield Phoenix, 2007.

Kim, Dohyung. "The Structure of Genesis 38: A Thematic Reading." *VT* 62 (2012): 550–560.

Klawans, Jonathan. *Purity, Sacrifice and the Temple: Symbolism and Supersessionism in the Study of Ancient Judaism.* Oxford: Oxford University Press, 2006.

Klein, Lillian R. "Hannah: Marginalized Victim and Social Redeemer." In *A Feminist Companion to Samuel and Kings,* edited by Athalya Brenner, 77–92. Sheffield, UK: Sheffield Academic, 1994.

Kramer, Samuel Noah. "Weeping Goddess: Sumerian Prototypes of the *Mater Dolorosa.*" *BA* 46 (1983): 69–79.

Lambert, David. "Fasting as a Penitential Rite: A Biblical Phenomenon?" *Harvard Theological Review* 96, no. 4 (2003): 477–512.

Leuchter, Mark. "Genesis 38 in Social and Historical Perspective." *JBL* 132, no. 2 (2013): 209–227.

Levenson, Jon D. *Esther.* Louisville: Westminster John Knox, 1997.

Levinson, Joshua. "An-Other Woman: Joseph and Potiphar's Wife. Staging the Body Politic." *JQR* 87, nos. 3–4 (1997): 269–301.

Macwilliam, Stuart. "Ideologies of Male Beauty and the Hebrew Bible." *BI* 17, no. 3 (2009): 265–287.

McCarter, P. Kyle, Jr. *I Samuel: A New Translation.* Anchor Bible 8. New York: Doubleday, 1980.

McKay, Heather A. "Confronting Redundancy as Middle Manager and Wife: The Feisty Woman of Genesis 39." *Semeia* 87 (1999): 215–231.

Meyers, Carol. "Hannah and Her Sacrifice: Reclaiming Female Agency." In *A Feminist Companion to Samuel and Kings,* edited by Athalya Brenner, 93–104. Sheffield, UK: Sheffield Academic, 1994.

———. *Rediscovering Eve: Ancient Israelite Women in Context.* Oxford: Oxford University Press, 2013.

Miller, Robert. "The Witch at the Navel of the World." *ZAW* 129, no. 1 (2017): 98–102.

Nicol, George G. "The Alleged Rape of Bathsheba: Some Observations on Ambiguity in Biblical Narrative." *JSOT* 73 (1997): 43–54.

Pirson, Ron. "The Twofold Message of Potiphar's Wife." *Scandinavian Journal of the Old Testament* 18, no. 2 (2004): 248–259.

Ruane, Nicole J. "Bathing, Status and Gender in Priestly Ritual." In *A Question of Sex? Gender and Difference in the Hebrew Bible and Beyond,* edited by Deborah W. Rooke, 66–81. Sheffield, UK: Sheffield Phoenix, 2007.

Schellekens, Jona. "Accession Days and Holidays: The Origins of the Jewish Festival of Purim." *JBL* 128, no. 1 (2009): 115–134.

Simon, Uriel. "The Stern Prophet and the Kind Witch." *Prooftexts* 8, no. 2 (1988): 159–171.

Stavrakopoulou, Francesca. "'Popular' Religion and 'Official' Religion: Practice, Perception, Portrayal." In *Religious Diversity in Ancient Israel and Judah*, edited by Francesca Stavrakopoulou and John Barton, 37–58. New York: T&T Clark, 2010.

Stiebert, Johanna. "The Wife of Potiphar, Sexual Harassment, and False Rape Allegations: Genesis 39 in Select Social Contexts of the Past and Present." In *The Bible and Gender Troubles in Africa*, edited by J. Kügler, R. Gabaitse, and J. Stiebert, 73–114. Bamberg: University of Bamberg Press, 2019.

Tamber-Rosenau, Caryn. "Biblical Bathing Beauties and the Manipulation of the Male Gaze." *JFSR* 33, no. 2 (2017): 55–72.

Trible, Phyllis. "Depatriarchalizing in Biblical Interpretation." *JAAR* 41, no. 1 (1973): 30–48.

———. "The Gift of a Poem: A Rhetorical Study of Jeremiah 31:15–22." *Andover Newton Quarterly* 17, no. 4 (1977): 271–280.

Washington, Harold G. "Violence and the Constructions of Gender in the Hebrew Bible: A New Historicist Approach." *BI* 5, no. 4 (1997): 324–363.

Westbrook, Raymond. *Property and the Family in Biblical Law*. Sheffield, UK: Sheffield Academic, 1991.

White, Sidnie Ann. "Esther: A Feminine Model for Jewish Diaspora." In *Gender and Difference in Ancient Israel*, edited by Peggy L. Day, 161–177. Minneapolis: Fortress, 1989.

Willis, Joyce, Andrew Pleffer, and Stephen Llewelyn. "Conversation in the Succession Narrative of Solomon." *VT* 61 (2011): 133–147.

Yee, Gale A. "Fraught with Background: Literary Ambiguity in II Samuel 11." *Interpretation* 42 (1988): 240–253.

GENERAL INDEX

SCRIPTURE INDEX

Exodus

Leviticus

Numbers

Deuteronomy

Job

Psalms

Proverbs

Ecclesiastes

Isaiah

Jeremiah